LEAVING CERTIFICATE

HIGHER AND ORDINARY LEVELS

COMPLETE
HOME ECONOMICS

FOOD STUDIES
ASSIGNMENT GUIDE

Leanne Gillick and Laura Healy

PUBLISHED BY:
Educate.ie
Walsh Educational Books Ltd
Castleisland, Co. Kerry, Ireland
www.educate.ie

EDITOR:
Carla Gallagher

DESIGN AND LAYOUT:
Liz White Designs

COVER DESIGN:
Kieran O'Donoghue

PRINTED AND BOUND BY:
Walsh Colour Print, Castleisland,
Co. Kerry, Ireland

PHOTOGRAPH ACKNOWLEDGEMENTS:
Bigstock, Shutterstock, StockFood and Tara
Fisher.

RECIPE ACKNOWLEDGEMENTS:
'Colcannon Soup with Parsley Pesto' from
Clodagh's Irish Kitchen by Clodagh McKenna.
Published by Kyle Books. Photography by Tara
Fisher.

'Happy Pear Dahl' from *The Happy Pear* by
David and Stephen Flynn. Published by Penguin.

The authors and publisher have made every
effort to trace all copyright holders. If any
have been overlooked, we would be happy to
make the necessary arrangements at the first
opportunity.

ISBN: 978-1-910468-62-3

INTRODUCTION

The *Complete Home Economics Food Studies Assignment Guide* is divided into two main sections:

 1 | **FOOD STUDIES PRACTICAL COURSEWORK JOURNAL (pages 4 to 80)**

This section explains each area of practice in detail. Sample answers are provided as a benchmark for your work for each area of practice. This will allow you to recognise the level of detail you will need to provide in order to obtain full marks.

Assignment templates are also provided (pages 57 to 80) in this section. You can use them to practise filling out your Food Studies Practical Coursework Journal.

 2 | **RECIPES (pages 81 to 143)**

The wide variety of recipes covers all areas of practice. The recipes will show you the level of detail that will be expected when you are completing the Implementation section of your Food Studies Practical Coursework Journal.

We hope you enjoy using this *Complete Home Economics Food Studies Assignment Guide*!

FOOD STUDIES PRACTICAL COURSEWORK JOURNAL

AN INTRODUCTION TO THE FOOD STUDIES PRACTICAL COURSEWORK JOURNAL

Introduction

- The Food Studies Practical Coursework Journal is a mandatory component of Leaving Certificate Home Economics. It accounts for **20%** of your overall mark.
- FIVE assignments will be issued to your school by the State Examinations Commission at the start of your two-year Leaving Certificate programme, along with a blank Food Studies Practical Coursework Journal.
- You are required to complete FOUR out of the FIVE assignments (all assignments are common to Higher Level and Ordinary Level).
- The completed Food Studies Practical Coursework Journal must be submitted for examination in November of your Leaving Certificate year.

Areas of Practice

The five assignments are from different Areas of Practice:
- TWO assignments are from Area of Practice A
- THREE assignments are from Areas of Practice B, C, D and E.

You can choose to complete any FOUR assignments.

Area of practice:	What it involves:
Area of Practice A Application of Nutritional Principles	Investigating the nutritional requirements and meal planning guidelines, and applying these in planning and preparing a suitable dish for those with: • Individual dietary requirements (e.g. children). **OR** • Special diets/modified diets (e.g. iron deficiency anaemia).
Area of Practice B Food Preparation and Cooking Processes	Investigating food preparation and cooking processes, and applying these in planning and preparing a dish that either: • Demonstrates the ability to follow specific food preparation and cooking processes (e.g. food safety practices). **OR** • Utilises new skills (e.g. using yeast). **OR** • Demonstrates the ability to use a specific item of equipment (e.g. a food processor).
Area of Practice C Food Technology	Investigating, producing and packaging new food products (e.g. preserves) using simple food processing procedures.
Area of Practice D Properties of a Food	Investigating the specific properties of food (e.g. aeration) and applying these in planning and preparing a dish.
Area of Practice E Comparative Analysis including Sensory Analysis	Investigating and using a sensory analysis test to either: • Compare two or more food products (e.g. different brands of crisps). **OR** • Carry out a sensory evaluation of a food (e.g. a nutritious breakfast cereal).

Recording Criteria

The Food Studies Practical Coursework Journal contains four blank assignments. Each assignment has an introductory page with space to record the chosen Area of Practice, the assignment number, your PPS number and the assignment brief. The rest of each assignment is laid out over five pages. You must record your information under four headings:

- Investigation: Analysis/Research
- Preparation and Planning
- Implementation
- Evaluation.

The information you give under each heading must meet the **recording criteria** in order to gain maximum marks. You will find the recording criteria at the beginning of your Food Studies Practical Coursework Journal. Take time to read and familiarise yourself with these before starting any assignment.

Marking Scheme

Each assignment is worth **80 marks** (5% of your overall result). The marks are allocated as follows:

- **Investigation: Analysis/Research: 32 marks**
- **Preparation and Planning: 8 marks**
- **Implementation: 28 marks**
- **Evaluation: 12 marks**

Please note that the breakdown of marks for each of the four headings mentioned above has not been released at the time of going to print. Your teacher will be able to tell you how the marks for each section will be allocated once the marking scheme has been released. Fill in the marks in the spaces below.

Investigation: Analysis/Research: 32 marks

Analysis and research: ☐ marks

Possible menu(s), dishes or food products: ☐ marks

Chosen dish/food product(s) and reasons for choice: ☐ marks

Sources of information: ☐ marks

Preparation and Planning: 8 marks

_____

_____

Implementation: 28 marks

Method/procedure: ☐ marks

Key factors: ☐ marks

Safety: ☐ marks

Hygiene: ☐ marks

Evaluation: 12 marks

Implementation: ☐ marks

Specific requirements: ☐ marks

Guidelines for Completing the Food Studies Practical Coursework Journal

The guidelines below highlight common errors and examples of good practice that should be considered when completing your Food Studies Practical Coursework Journal. Many of the guidelines have been adapted from the Chief Examiners' reports from 2004, 2007 and 2011.

Before you fill in your journal:

- Read each assignment brief carefully and highlight the key requirements. For example:

> **Nutritional awareness and a positive approach to healthy eating are important factors for young people who participate in active sport.**
>
> Research and elaborate on the **nutritional needs** and the **meal planning guidelines** that should be considered when planning meals for **young people who participate in active sport**. Having regard to the factors identified in your research, suggest a **range of two-course menus** suitable for the **main meal** of the day for this group of young people. Prepare, cook and serve **one of the main courses** from your research. **Evaluate** the assignment in terms of (a) **implementation** and (b) the **specific requirements** of the assignment.

- Study and research the topic in the assignment brief before starting. This will allow you to provide detailed and well-explained information in your assignment, and to demonstrate a clear understanding of the topic.

- Research information from a variety of sources (e.g. websites and books), not just from your textbook for the Investigation: Analysis/Research section of each assignment. This will allow you to write about the topic in detail.
- Choose a challenging recipe for each assignment to demonstrate a progression in skill level from the Junior Certificate.
- Do not repeat or partially modify recipes across assignments. For example, marks will be lost if you choose a vegetable stir-fry in Assignment 1 and a chicken stir-fry in Assignment 2.

When filling in your journal:

- Do not use a pencil. Always use a black or blue ballpoint pen.
- Check the page heading to make sure that you are on the correct page before adding information. If you record your information on the wrong page, marks will be lost.
- Avoid leaving unnecessary spaces or blank lines on pages.
- Write clearly on the lines. Do not draw extra answer lines in your journal.
- Use clear headings and include numbers or bullet points where necessary to make your assignments easier for the examiner to read and correct.
- Researched information must not be copied directly from the source from which it was obtained. It must be written in your own words to show that you understand the topic. Also, your Food Studies Practical Coursework Journal must not be the same as anyone else's.
- Follow the recording criteria very carefully and make sure that all of the criteria are met. You will find the recording criteria at the beginning of your Food Studies Practical Coursework Journal.
- Complete each assignment fully before starting the next assignment. This will prevent you from mixing up assignments.
- Do not add extra pages to your journal or enclose any additional material.

We will look at the Areas of Practice in more detail in the next section (pages 9 to 44).

AREAS OF PRACTICE A, B, C, D AND E

The introduction included information on the five Areas of Practice, the recording criteria and the marking scheme. It also provided guidelines on how to successfully complete your Food Studies Practical Coursework Journal.

We will now look at the key requirements of Areas of Practice A, B, C, D and E in more detail and will explore the main points that need to be addressed for each Area of Practice.

> Certain recording criteria are **common** to all Areas of Practice. They will be covered in the 'Common Topics in All Areas of Practice' section (pages 45 to 56).

Please note that sections of Sample Answers are included in this guide. The Sample Answers are used to illustrate relevant points and they do not cover all of the points required to secure full marks for the assignment.

Area of Practice A: Application of Nutritional Principles

Two assignments are issued for Area of Practice A. Depending on the assignment, this will involve investigating the nutritional requirements and meal planning guidelines and applying these in the planning and preparation of a suitable dish for those with:

- Individual dietary requirements (e.g. children).

OR

- Special diets/modified diets (e.g. iron deficiency anaemia).

Key Requirements of Area of Practice A

When answering an assignment from Area of Practice A, you may be expected to:

- Research the risk factors associated with the special diet/modified diet specified in the assignment.
- Research the nutritional needs of the individual or group specified in the assignment.
- Research the meal planning guidelines specific to the individual or group.
- Plan a menu(s) or list main course dishes suited to the individual or group.
- Choose a dish to prepare, using the knowledge you have gained through your research, suited to the individual group. Outline two reasons for your choice.
- Prepare, cook and evaluate your chosen dish.

These key requirements may differ depending on the assignment specifications. Make sure to read the assignment brief carefully and highlight the key requirements. This will help you to lay out all of the necessary points under the correct headings. We will now look at what should be included under each heading area for Area of Practice A.

Investigation: Analysis/Research (32 marks)

Analysis and Research

Begin by introducing the individual or group you have been asked to investigate in the assignment. For example:

 Nutritional awareness and a positive approach to healthy eating are important for young people who participate in active sport. (2016)

A young, active sportsperson has specific nutritional and dietary needs that should be met in order for them to reach their full potential. Their diet can have a profound impact on both their athletic performance and growth levels.

Some assignments may also ask you to investigate a specific point that will be outlined in the key requirements of the assignment. This should be included after the introduction. For example:

 Research from the World Health Organization has found that Ireland has the highest death rate from heart disease in people under 65 in the EU. With reference to the above statement, identify the risk factors associated with poor cardiovascular health. (2014)

Risk factors associated with poor cardiovascular health:

Modifiable Risk Factors	Non-modifiable Risk Factors
Hypertension (high blood pressure)	Age
Smoking/excessive alcohol consumption	Gender
Diabetes	Family history
Physical inactivity/stress/anger	Race
Unhealthy diet (e.g. high intake of saturated fat and salt)	Post-menopausal
High cholesterol/obesity	

Nutritional Needs

In this section, you must document the relevant nutritional needs of the specified individual or group under the following headings:

✓ Reference Intake (RI)/Recommended Daily Allowance (RDA)

✓ Food sources

✓ Functions suited to the individual or group.

You should research the following nutrients:

- **Protein:** HBV (high biological value) and LBV (low biological value)
- **Fat:** saturated and unsaturated
- **Carbohydrate:** sugar, starch and dietary fibre
- **Water-soluble Vitamins:** C and B-group
- **Fat-soluble Vitamins:** A, D, E and K
- **Minerals:** Iron, calcium and others
- **Water**.

TIP If the assignment brief provides additional information about the specified individual or group, you must refer to this information when writing about nutritional needs and meal planning guidelines (e.g. **young people who participate in active sport**).

TIP Refer to the energy requirements of the specified individual or group when you are writing about carbohydrates.

Always refer to the individual or group specified in the assignment brief under <u>each</u> nutrient heading. For example:

 Research and elaborate on the nutritional needs that should be considered when planning meals for children aged between two and five years. (2017)

Protein

Reference Intake (RI): a child (aged 2 to 5) requires 30-50 g of protein each day from both high biological value (HBV) and low biological value (LBV) sources. This should account for 10-15% of a child's daily calorie intake.

Food sources: HBV food sources include lean meat, fish, poultry, eggs, milk or cheese. LBV food sources include nuts, seeds or pulses. HBV are more beneficial than LBV as they contain all essential amino acids.

Functions: children require protein for growth, as childhood is a time of rapid cell growth and development. They also require protein for repair of body tissues (e.g. a cut on the skin).

(Please note that this is only a sample of what is required. Further detail is required for this answer.)

Meal Planning Guidelines

Next, you must research and document the meal planning guidelines that should be followed when planning meals for the specified individual or group. Read the points below and research and write about the ones that are relevant to the individual or group.

- **Food pyramid:** List the types of foods and number of servings that the specified individual or group should consume from each shelf of the food pyramid. Explain the importance of following the food pyramid when planning meals.

- **Healthy eating guidelines:** Outline the healthy eating guidelines that apply to the specified individual or group. For example, when planning meals for individuals who wish to reduce their weight, it is recommended that they eat lean meat, poultry and fish (oily is preferred) instead of high-fat or processed meats in order to help reduce their saturated fat intake.

- **Specific dietary requirements:** Outline the specific dietary requirements that should be considered when meal planning for the specified individual or group. For example, when planning meals for older people, include high biological value (HBV) protein foods such as fish, eggs and milk, as they are required for the repair of damaged or worn cells. Protein foods included should be easy to chew and digest.

- **Resources:** List the resources (e.g. time, money, equipment) available to the specified individual or group and explain how these resources might affect the planning of meals. For example, when planning meals for a family on a low income, choose dishes carefully in order to meet the family's nutritional needs within their budget.

- **Availability of food:** Explain how the availability of food might affect the meals being planned for the specified individual or group. For example, when planning meals for a family with a range of dietary needs, consider the availability of seasonal food and ease of access to specialised ingredients.

- **Number of people:** State how the number of people being catered for will affect meal planning. For example, when planning a meal for an individual rather than a group (e.g. a family), the recipe may have to be modified, as many recipes cater for four people.
- **Preferences:** Outline the importance of considering the preferences of the specified individual or group when meal planning. For example, when planning meals for a child, consider their likes and dislikes to ensure they achieve a balanced diet, as some children are fussy eaters.

Always refer to the individual or group specified in the assignment brief under <u>each</u> meal planning guideline heading. For example:

 Research and elaborate on the meal planning guidelines that should be considered when planning meals for children aged between two and five years. (2017)

The food pyramid:

When planning meals for a child (aged 2 to 5), it is important to use the food pyramid to ensure they are receiving the correct amount of food or the correct number of servings: bread, cereal and potatoes (6 servings), fruit and vegetables (5 servings), dairy (5 servings), protein (2 servings) and limited amounts of reduced-fat spreads and oils. Foods that are high in fat, sugar and salt should not be eaten every day. To ensure balance, meals should contain foods from a minimum of three of the main food groups.

The healthy eating guidelines:

The healthy eating guidelines encourage people to limit the consumption of food and drink from the top shelf of the food pyramid (e.g. biscuits and cakes) as these are high in fat, sugar and salt. Overconsumption of these foods is leading to an increase in the number of children (aged 2 to 5) with childhood obesity, type 2 diabetes and dental decay. Parents should limit sugary or high-fat snacks and include healthy alternatives in their place (e.g. nuts, yoghurt). Sugary drinks should be replaced with plenty of water or milk to prevent dehydration.

(Please note that this is only a sample of what is required. Further detail is required for this answer.)

Possible Menu(s)/Dishes

Each assignment in Area of Practice A will ask you to plan a menu(s) or list dishes which meet the nutritional needs and follow the meal planning guidelines of the individual or group specified in the assignment. Please note:

- All menus or dishes listed should be balanced (including a minimum of three of the main food groups).
- If asked to draw up a menu(s), it should always be drawn up in a box, using the menu format.

The example below shows you how to list suitable dishes.

 Healthy meal plans do not have to be complicated or expensive and should be suitable for the whole family to enjoy. Investigate a range of main course dishes suitable for the main meal of the day for a family who want to eat healthy, uncomplicated and inexpensive meals. (2014)

Main meals for a family who want to eat healthy, uncomplicated and inexpensive meals:

- **Spaghetti and meatballs** in a tomato and basil sauce, made with lean mince and topped with grated cheese.
- **Chicken curry** made with fresh vegetables, served on a bed of wholegrain rice, with a green salad and garlic naan bread.
- **Fish cakes** made with mashed potato, salmon and cod, baked and served with homemade sweet potato wedges and roasted Mediterranean vegetables.
- **Mac 'n' Cheese** made with a homemade cheese roux sauce, including chicken and cauliflower and served with a green salad.

The following example shows you how to plan a menu:

 Having regard to the factors identified in your research, write a menu (three meals) for one day for a person who wishes to improve his/her cardiovascular health. (2014)

Menu for a person who wishes to improve their cardiovascular health

BREAKFAST:
- Porridge made with cholesterol-lowering milk topped with sunflower seeds.
- Orange and grapefruit segments topped with cholesterol-lowering yoghurt.
- A cup of herbal tea.

LUNCH:
- A wholemeal wrap filled with lettuce, tomato, grilled chicken and low-fat cheese.
- A bowl of tomato and basil soup.
- A glass of water.

DINNER:
Starter:
- Spinach and rocket salad with cherry tomatoes, grilled peppers and baby beetroot.

Main Course:
- Thai salmon fishcakes with quinoa salad and sweet potato wedges.
- A glass of skimmed milk.

SNACKS:
- Crudités (carrot, celery and red pepper strips) with low-fat hummus.
- Kale and banana smoothie with chia seeds.

Chosen Dish and Reasons for Choice

Go to page 46 of 'Common Topics in All Areas of Practice' for information on how to complete this section.

Sources of Information

Go to page 47 of 'Common Topics in All Areas of Practice' for information on how to complete this section.

Preparation and Planning (8 marks)

Go to page 47 of 'Common Topics in All Areas of Practice' for information on how to complete this section.

Implementation (28 marks)

Go to page 48 of 'Common Topics in All Areas of Practice' for information on how to complete this section.

Evaluation (12 marks)

Evaluation of Implementation

Go to page 51 of 'Common Topics in All Areas of Practice' for information on how to complete this section.

Evaluation of the Specific Requirements

In this section, you must outline:

- How your chosen dish meets the nutritional requirements of the individual or group specified in the assignment.

AND

- How your chosen dish adheres to the meal planning guidelines for the individual or group specified in the assignment.

For example:

 Identify and elaborate on the nutritional needs and the meal planning guidelines that should be considered when planning meals for a low-income family. Evaluate the assignment in terms of the specific requirements of the assignment. (2010)

Nutritional Requirements:

My cottage pie dish met the nutritional requirements of a family with a limited income. It was suitable for a main meal and was nutritionally balanced as it contained foods from all four food groups. The potatoes contained carbohydrates. This provided the family with a source of energy. The vegetables (diced carrots and frozen peas) contained vitamins A and C. These are important for eyesight and healthy gums. The milk in the mashed potato and the cheese topping provided calcium and vitamin D, for healthy bones and teeth. The lean mince provided protein, for growth, and iron, for the production of red blood cells. Therefore, I feel my cottage pie did meet the nutritional needs of both the younger and older members of the family.

Meal Planning Guidelines:

As this family has a limited food budget, I took particular care when deciding on a dish that would meet the meal planning guidelines, i.e. a low-cost, nutritious dish that would appeal to the whole family. I made sure that the dish chosen was cost-effective and could be prepared on a limited budget. The overall price of the cottage pie was only €5.34. This is great value, considering it is sufficient to feed a family of four. All of the ingredients can be purchased in a low-cost supermarket. It can be made in bulk and frozen for future meals. It is a dish all family members would enjoy. Therefore, I feel I have met the specific meal planning requirements of this assignment.

MY PERSONAL NOTES:
Area of Practice A: Application of Nutritional Principles

(Use this space to take notes during class or to record your personal research on Area of Practice A.)

_____

_____

_____

_____

_____

_____

_____

_____

_____

_____

_____

_____

_____

_____

_____

_____

_____

_____

_____

_____

_____

_____

_____

_____

_____

_____

_____

_____

_____

_____

_____

_____

_____

_____

_____

_____

_____

_____

_____

_____

_____

_____

_____

_____

_____

_____

_____

_____

_____

_____

_____

_____

_____

_____

_____

_____

_____

_____

_____

Area of Practice B: Food Preparation and Cooking Processes

One assignment **may** be issued for Area of Practice B. This will involve investigating food preparation and cooking processes and applying these in planning and preparing a dish that either:

• Demonstrates the ability to follow specific food preparation or cooking processes (e.g. food safety practices, roasting).

OR

• Develops a new skill (e.g. using yeast).

OR

• Demonstrates the ability to use a specific item of equipment (e.g. a food processor).

Key Requirements of Area of Practice B

If the assignment is related to **food preparation or cooking processes**, you may be expected to:

• Identify the food preparation or cooking process and explain its importance.
• List the key points that should be observed to ensure success in adhering to the food preparation or cooking process.
• List dishes that illustrate the food preparation or cooking process.
• Choose a dish to prepare, using the knowledge you have gained through your research. Outline two reasons for your choice.
• Prepare, cook and evaluate your chosen dish.

If the assignment is related to **the development of a new skill**, you may be expected to:

• Identify the skill outlined in the assignment brief.
• Identify the products associated with the skill and outline the different types or varieties of these products.
• Explain how the skill is used in food preparation and the underlying principle involved in its use.

- List the key points that should be observed to ensure success in carrying out your chosen skill.
- List dishes that illustrate the use of the skill.
- Choose a dish to prepare, using the knowledge you have gained through your research. Outline two reasons for your choice.
- Prepare, cook and evaluate your chosen dish.

If the assignment is related to **the use of a specific item of equipment**, you may be expected to:

- Research the different types of the specific item of equipment, as outlined in the assignment brief.
- Outline the uses of the equipment.
- Explain the working principle of the equipment.
- List the key points that should be observed to ensure success when using this equipment.
- List dishes that illustrate the use of the equipment.
- Choose a dish to prepare, using the knowledge you have gained through your research. Outline two reasons for your choice.
- Prepare, cook and evaluate your chosen dish.

These key requirements may differ depending on the assignment specifications. Make sure to read the assignment brief carefully and highlight the key requirements. This will help you to lay out all of the necessary points under the correct headings. We will now look at what should be included under each heading area for Area of Practice B.

Investigation: Analysis/Research (32 marks)

Analysis and Research

Begin by introducing the topic you have been asked to investigate in the assignment. For example:

Assignment Area – Development of a New Skill:

 Carry out research on commercially prepared filo pastry or commercially prepared puff pastry. (2005)

Certain types of pastry, such as filo or puff pastry, require a lot of time and skill to prepare. Often, only skilled pastry chefs will have the necessary resources to make them. For this reason, commercially bought versions are hugely beneficial to the everyday consumer.

The layout of your investigation will depend on the key requirements of the assignment. For example:

Assignment Area – Food Preparation or Cooking Processes:

 Roasting adds flavour to food when used as a method of cooking. Carry out research on roasting as a method of cooking. (2007)

Roasting is a method of cooking meat or vegetables by radiant/convection heat in front of or over a glowing source of heat. Food is cooked by convection in a hot oven where hot air rises and cold air falls to create an even temperature. A small amount of fat is used in roasting (basted over the food during cooking)

to brown the meat, keep food moist, give flavour and prevent burning. Food may also be rotated on a spit or rotisserie. Roasting can either take place in an open tin for better colour and flavour or can be covered to reduce shrinkage.

(Please note that this is only a sample of what is required. Further detail is required for this answer.)

 Consumers need to be well informed on food safety practices when purchasing, storing and preparing food. They should know common food safety hazards and how to manage food safety. Carry out research on dishes that require special adherence to safe food practices. (2017)

Dishes that require special adherence to safe food practices:

- Spaghetti and meatballs
- Beef burgers and potato wedges
- Chicken and mushroom puff pastry pie
- Chicken fillet stuffed with sage and onion stuffing and roasted vegetables
- Mixed seafood paella.

Assignment Area – Development of a New Skill:

 Rough puff and choux are two types of pastry frequently used in home baking. Compare and contrast rough puff and choux pastry having regard to key points to follow to ensure success when making each pastry and the underlying principles involved. (2013)

Key points that should be observed to ensure success when making choux pastry:

- Measure ingredients accurately. Too much liquid will make the pastry too runny and too little means that the batter will be thick and will not allow the buns to puff up. Too much egg leads to a stiff outer layer and too little egg leads to a thin and fragile layer.
- Always use strong flour, as the extra gluten strengthens the dough.
- Do not boil the water before the butter is melted, as boiling water will evaporate while waiting for the butter to melt. This will reduce the proportion of water and affect the end result.

(Please note that this is only a sample of what is required. Further detail is required for this answer.)

 Gelatine (gelatin) has a wide range of uses both culinary and in food manufacture. Carry out research on gelatine in relation to the following: dishes that illustrate the use of gelatine. (2014)

- Oreo cheesecake
- Chocolate mousse
- Whoopie pies with marshmallow filling
- Lemon panna cotta with raspberry coulis
- Savoury chicken pie
- Liver paté.

Assignment Area – Use of a Specific Item of Equipment:

 Research the different types and varied uses of food processors. (2006)

Type/Brand	Cost	Description
Kenwood FPP225 Multipro Food Processor	€66.99	• 750 watts • 2 speeds and pulse function • 1.2 litre main bowl liquid working capacity • Functions/Uses: 　— Slices, grates, whisks, dices, crushes ice 　— Safety interlock system.
Magimix 4200XL Food Processor – Stainless Steel	€390	• 950 watts • 2 speeds and pulse function • 1.3 litre main bowl liquid working capacity • Functions/Uses: 　— Slices, grates, whisks, kneads dough, crushes ice 　— Safety interlock system.

(Please note that this is only a sample of what is required. Further detail is required for this answer.)

 Select either a wok or a steamer and research uses, i.e. dishes/foods, including main course dishes, that can be cooked using this item of equipment. (2008)

- Steamed fillet of salmon with a Thai marinade, served with steamed baby potatoes, julienne carrots and asparagus.
- Steamed Cajun-style chicken fillet, served on a bed of mashed potatoes (steamed) and steamed green beans.
- Steamed fresh prawns, served with a sweet chilli dipping sauce, a large steamed potato filled with sour cream, steamed spinach and a corn on the cob.
- Steamed fillet of haddock with grated ginger, served with steamed artichoke, fresh peas and a side of steamed baby potatoes.

Possible Dishes

In this section, you must list possible dishes that meet the key requirements of the assignment, one of which must be your chosen dish. For example:

 Gelatine (gelatin) has a wide range of uses both culinary and in food manufacture. (2014)

For this assignment I could make an Oreo cheesecake **or** a lemon panna cotta with raspberry coulis.

Chosen Dish and Reasons for Choice

Go to page 46 of 'Common Topics in All Areas of Practice' for information on how to complete this section.

Sources of Information

Go to page 47 of 'Common Topics in All Areas of Practice' for information on how to complete this section.

Preparation and Planning (8 marks)

Go to page 47 of 'Common Topics in All Areas of Practice' for information on how to complete this section.

Implementation (28 marks)

Go to page 48 of 'Common Topics in All Areas of Practice' for information on how to complete this section.

Evaluation (12 marks)

Evaluation of Implementation

Go to page 51 of 'Common Topics in All Areas of Practice' for information on how to complete this section.

Evaluation of the Specific Requirements

In this section, you must (depending on the key requirements of the assignment):

- Evaluate how adhering to the food preparation process (e.g. food safety practices) or the cooking process (e.g. roasting) ensured the success of the dish.

OR

- Outline the advantages and/or disadvantages of using an item of equipment (e.g. food processor) or carrying out a new skill (e.g. using yeast).
  Note: You can give one advantage and one disadvantage or two advantages or two disadvantages.

OR

- Evaluate your success in achieving a desired result in the development of a new skill (e.g. a light, airy texture in a soufflé).

Depending on the assignment, you may also be asked to carry out a cost comparison between your dish and a similar commercial product.

The example below shows you how to evaluate how adhering to the cooking process ensured the success of the dish:

 Roasting adds flavour to food when used as a method of cooking. Evaluate the assignment in terms of roasting as a method of cooking. (2007)

I chose to quick roast my stuffed chicken fillets at 220 °C for 15 minutes and then reduced the temperature to 180 °C for a further 10 minutes. When I took the fillets out of the oven the surface of the chicken was golden brown due to the high temperatures and hot fat used. This created an appetising finish. When I cut into the fillets they were succulent and juicy as I had taken care to baste them at regular intervals. The stuffing also helped to retain the moisture and prevent them from drying out. The hot fat and high temperatures during roasting added to the overall flavour. Overall I found this to be an easy method of cooking. I only had to baste it a few times after I put it in the oven, but otherwise it cooked with little attention needed.

The following example shows you how to outline the advantages/disadvantages of carrying out a new skill and how to carry out a cost comparison:

 BRIEF **The variety of yeast breads available to consumers has increased in recent years. Evaluate the assignment in terms of (i) the advantages and disadvantages of making yeast products at home and (ii) cost in comparison to a similar commercial product. (2010)**

(i) Advantage: The main advantage of yeast is how easy it is to use. This was my first time using yeast to make my own bread and I was so surprised at how easy the process was. Once I mastered providing the correct conditions (e.g. warmth) and had put aside enough time, it was a straightforward and simple process. I knew I had been successful because the dough doubled in size during proving and rose well in the oven. I am now confident that I could try this at home. Another advantage of using yeast to make bread is that it does not require any specialised skills or equipment, making it easy for anyone to do.

Disadvantage: The only disadvantage to making your own yeast products is the time involved. If you have a few hours to spare, it is enjoyable. But it is not suitable for those in a hurry or for those who are short on time. It takes time to knead, prove, knock back, prove again and bake. This is the only thing that would put me off doing this at home.

(ii) Cost in comparison to a similar commercial product:
I was very surprised at how cheap it is to make your own yeast bread. It required just a few simple ingredients: flour, yeast, salt and water. My bread cost only 69c, whereas a similar loaf of yeast bread from my local deli cost €2.99. This amounted to a saving of €2.30! If people are looking for ways in which to reduce their weekly shopping bill, I strongly suggest that they start to make their own bread at home.

The example below shows you how to outline your success in achieving a desired result in the development of a new skill:

 BRIEF **Prepare, make and serve a hot or cold soufflé of your choice. Evaluate the assignment in terms of success in achieving a light aerated texture. (2009)**

When I finished whisking the egg whites for the soufflé, I could see that they had more than doubled in size. The bubbles of air were easy to see and the mixture looked light and airy. I knew I had followed all the steps correctly to ensure I achieved a light and airy mixture. I took care to fold the egg white into the mixture gently to prevent the loss of any air bubbles.

After cooking, I removed the soufflé from the oven. I was delighted that it had risen 2 cm above the rim of the ramekin. This showed that I had incorporated plenty of air during the mixing process. When the soufflé was cooking, these air bubbles expanded, resulting in the soufflé rising. When I tasted the soufflé, it was bubbly and light in texture. Overall, I'm delighted with how well the soufflé turned out and I believe I achieved the desired texture.

MY PERSONAL NOTES:
Area of Practice B: Food Preparation and Cooking Processes

(Use this space to take notes during class or to record your personal research on Area of Practice B.)

Area of Practice C: Food Technology

One assignment **may** be issued for Area of Practice C. This will involve investigating, producing and packaging new food products (e.g. preserves) using simple food processing procedures.

Key Requirements of Area of Practice C

If you choose an assignment from Area of Practice C, you may be expected to:

- Investigate and research the range of commercially available food products outlined in the assignment brief.
- Research the ingredients used in the making of the food product outlined in the assignment brief.
- Explain the underlying principles involved in making the food product.
- Outline the method involved in the making of the food product.
- Detail potential problems that may arise in the making of this food product and ways of preventing these problems from occurring.
- Give details of the containers, covers and labels required to package the food product.
- List possible examples of the food product suitable for this assignment.
- Choose a food product to prepare using the knowledge you have gained through your research. Outline two reasons for your choice.
- Outline how you would serve your chosen food product.
- Prepare, cook and evaluate your chosen food product.

These key requirements may differ depending on the assignment specifications. Make sure to read the assignment brief carefully and highlight the key requirements. This will help you to lay out all of the necessary points under the correct headings. We will now look at what should be included under each heading area for Area of Practice C.

Investigation: Analysis/Research (32 marks)

Analysis and Research

Begin the investigation by introducing the topic you have been asked to investigate in the assignment. For example:

 Fruit and vegetables in season can be preserved by using them to make chutney and relishes. (2007)

Chutneys and relishes are gaining in popularity due to the high-quality homemade products being sold in local farmers markets. Chutneys and relishes can add flavour and texture to cold meats and sandwiches, transforming them into gastronomic delights.

The layout of your investigation will depend on the key requirements of the assignment. For example:

 A wide range of yoghurts are available on the market for the consumer to choose from. Carry out research on the range of commercially available yoghurts. (2009)

Brands	Range	Flavours
Yoplait, Danone, Onken, Müller, Glenisk, Benecol, Rachel's Organic, Yeo Valley and supermarket own-brand yoghurts (e.g. Tesco)	Set, stirred, custard-style, natural, fruit-flavoured, bio, functional, thick and creamy with separate fruit section, yoghurt drinks, frozen yoghurt and low-fat/diet	Raspberry, strawberry, blueberry, mixed berries, rhubarb, lemon, peach, coconut, chocolate, hazelnut and prune

 The market for handmade sweets and chocolates has expanded significantly in recent years. Carry out research on commercially available handmade sweets and chocolates. (2008)

	Sweets	Chocolates
Brands	Oatfield, Pandora Bell, Shandon, Lemon's, Athlone	Butlers, Lily O'Brien's, Lir, Leonidas, Chocolate Garden of Ireland, Skelligs, Bean and Goose, Áine, Wilkies, Ó Conaill
Types	Boiled, toffees, marzipan, peppermint creams, fudge, cream fondants, Turkish delight, nougat	Milk/dark/white, moulded, truffles, filled (e.g. orange, strawberry and liqueur)

 Investigate the different fruits and vegetables that can be preserved by chutney and relish making. (2012)

Fruits	Vegetables
Apples, pears, apricots, plums, rhubarb, bananas, raisins, sultanas, dates, damsons, gooseberries, mangos, nectarines, cranberries, blackberries, dates, pumpkins, coconuts, papayas and pineapples	Tomatoes, red & green peppers, marrows, garlic, beetroot, corn kernels, cabbages, shallots, chillies, cucumbers, cauliflowers, fennel, green beans and onions

Carry out research on the rise in popularity of home baking. (2011)

Home-baked foods taste far better than any commercial product. They are fresher and are superior in quality. Baking at home is much cheaper than buying a commercially produced product. For example, it can cost €2.99 for a single iced cupcake in a coffee shop or deli, whereas it can cost as little as 24c to make your own.

(Please note that this is only a sample of what is required. Further detail is required for this answer.)

 Carry out research on making preserves (jam, jellies and marmalades) in relation to the underlying principles involved. (2013)

The underlying principles involved in jam making:

Fruit is boiled to 100 °C. The heat destroys enzymes and microorganisms that could cause the jam to spoil, as their optimum temperature is 37 °C. The high temperature also softens the fruit by breaking down its cell walls.

Then 65% sugar is added. This inhibits the growth of microbes by surrounding the microbial cells with a concentrated sugar solution that draws water out of the cells by osmosis. This dehydrates the microbial cells and causes them to die.

Sealing the jam is important to prevent the re-entry of microorganisms.

 Using your choice of fruit/vegetables, prepare and pot a chutney or relish. Include details of the container and the labelling you used. (2007)

Details of containers used when potting chutney:

- Glass jars that are washed, rinsed and sterilised.
- The jars may be sealed with one of the following: a screw-top lacquered or plastic-coated lid, vinegar-proof paper, freezer bags or greaseproof paper with a circle of cotton fabric dipped in wax.

Details of labels used when potting chutney:

- Labels with the product name (e.g. Tomato and Red Pepper Chutney) and the date of manufacture (e.g. 18th November 2016).

Possible Food Products

In this section, you must list possible examples of the food product that meet the key requirements of the assignment, one of which must be your chosen food product. For example:

 The market for handmade sweets and chocolates has expanded significantly in recent years. From your research, prepare and make one of the products that you have investigated. (2008)

For this assignment I could make a dark chocolate truffle with a ganache centre **or** a milk chocolate cup with a strawberry filling.

Chosen Food Product and Reasons for Choice

Go to page 46 of 'Common Topics in All Areas of Practice' for information on how to complete this section.

Sources of Information

Go to page 47 of 'Common Topics in All Areas of Practice' for information on how to complete this section.

Preparation and Planning (8 marks)

Go to page 47 of 'Common Topics in All Areas of Practice' for information on how to complete this section.

Implementation (28 marks)

Go to page 48 of 'Common Topics in All Areas of Practice' for information on how to complete this section.

Evaluation (12 marks)

Evaluation of Implementation

Go to page 51 of 'Common Topics in All Areas of Practice' for information on how to complete this section.

Evaluation of the Specific Requirements

In this section, you must:

- Evaluate the practicality of making the food product at home (i.e. Is it worth the effort?). In this answer, you could make reference to:
  - Cost
  - Time
  - Skills
  - Equipment
  - Packaging and storage.

Depending on the assignment, you may also be asked to carry out a cost comparison comparing your product to a similar commercial variety, or to evaluate the cost-effectiveness of the product.

The example below shows you how to evaluate the assignment in terms of practicality:

 Home baking is becoming increasingly popular for many different reasons. Prepare and bake one of the products (either muffins or cupcakes) that you have investigated. Evaluate the assignment in terms of practicability of home baking. (2011)

Skills: Baking cupcakes at home requires a certain level of skill. It is not something that everyone can carry out successfully. When making cupcakes, the ingredients must be measured correctly and combined to make a light batter. Icing the cupcakes with a piping bag can be difficult. For this reason, it might not be practical for unskilled bakers to make cupcakes. It might be easier to buy them from a shop, although they will have to pay a lot more!

Equipment: No specialised equipment is needed to make cupcakes. If you have a bowl, wooden spoon, sieve and bun tray, you should be able to make cupcakes successfully. If you do not have a piping bag, you can simply ice them using a knife. In this regard, cupcakes are a practical option for home cooks.

The following example shows you how to evaluate the assignment in terms of cost effectiveness:

 A variety of fruits can be preserved by boiling and the addition of sugar. Prepare and pot two varieties of fruit preserves. Evaluate the assignment in terms of cost effectiveness. (2004)

I picked the blackberries from my local hedgerows and collected apples from the tree in the garden. Therefore the only cost incurred was the sugar and lemon. They cost me only €1.56 in total. I made 8 jars of jam. Therefore, it only cost 19c per jar. A jar of Chivers jam costs approximately €2.46. Therefore I saved €2.27 by making it myself. Making homemade jam is much cheaper, so in my opinion it is worth the effort.

MY PERSONAL NOTES:
Area of Practice C: Food Technology

(Use this space to take notes during class or to record your personal research on Area of Practice C.)

Area of Practice D: Properties of a Food

One assignment **may** be issued for Area of Practice D. This will involve investigating the specific properties of a food (e.g. aeration).

Key Requirements of Area of Practice D

If you choose an assignment from Area of Practice D, you may be expected to:

- Define the property/properties outlined in the assignment brief.
- Explain the reasons why the property/properties are used in food preparation/cooking.
- Outline the causes of the property/properties.
- List a range of dishes that illustrate the culinary application of the property/properties.
- Explain the underlying principle of the property/properties.
- List possible examples of dishes suitable for this assignment.
- Choose a dish, using the knowledge you have gained through your research. Outline two reasons for your choice.
- Prepare, cook and evaluate your chosen dish.

These key requirements may differ depending on the assignment specifications. Make sure to read the assignment brief carefully and highlight the key requirements. This will help you to lay out all of the necessary points under the correct headings. We will now look at what should be included under each heading area for Area of Practice D.

Investigation: Analysis/Research (32 marks)

Analysis and Research

Begin by introducing the topic you have been asked to investigate in the assignment. For example:

 Eggs have a wide variety of culinary uses attributable to their properties. (2012)

Eggs have many useful properties including coagulation, foam formation/aeration and emulsification. These are commonly used to create many wonderful sweet and savoury dishes.

The layout of your investigation will depend on the key requirements of the assignment. See the examples below:

 Define caramelisation or coagulation. (2008)

Caramelisation is a form of non-enzymatic browning. When sugar is heated, it melts and produces a brown syrup called caramel. There are 10 gradual stages between sugar melting and caramelisation occurring. These occur between 104 °C and 177 °C. Caramelisation normally occurs at 160 °C. It results in an attractive brown colour, a pleasant smell and a bittersweet taste.

 Many popular recipes specify the use of a marinade. Carry out research on the reasons for using marinades in food preparation. (2013)

Marinating is used to:

- Add to/improve the flavour of food (e.g. garlic and chilli salmon with beef).
- Tenderise meat (e.g. pork chops). The acid component of the marinade (e.g. wine, vinegar, citrus fruits) converts the collagen in connective tissue to gelatine, making it easier to digest.
- Make use of lesser quality/cheaper cuts of meat (e.g. round steak), as marinades tenderise the meat and make it easier to digest.
- Make food juicer by adding moisture (e.g. pork satay wet marinade/rub).
- Help make food healthier (e.g. marinating meat in lemon juice or vinegar reduces carcinogenic compounds produced by grilling).

Caramelisation and coagulation are used in food preparation to enhance the properties of the final dish/product. Investigate and elaborate on the application of caramelisation or coagulation in the making of a range of dishes, explaining the principle involved. (2008)

The underlying principle of coagulation:

- When heated, the protein in eggs sets or coagulates.
- Proteins in the egg white coagulate between 60 °C and 65 °C, causing the egg white to become opaque and solid. Proteins in the egg yolk coagulate between 65 °C and 70 °C.
- This is an example of protein denaturation as the nature of the protein chain is irreversibly changed. Heat causes the tertiary (3D) structure of a protein to unravel, straighten and bond together around small pockets of water.

The culinary applications of coagulation:

Quiche Lorraine, Mediterranean quiche, lemon meringue pie, lemon curd tartlets, soufflé, omelette, egg custard, custard tarts, bread and butter pudding.

(Please note that this is only a sample of what is required. Further detail is required for this answer.)

 Fats and oils have a wide variety of culinary uses, attributable to their properties, when used in food preparation. Identify dishes that illustrate the use of each property identified. (2010)

Property	Flavour absorption	Plasticity	Shortening	Effects of heat	Emulsification
Dishes that illustrate the use of identified properties	• Garlic butter on homemade yeast bread • Chilli-infused olive oil (used in a stir-fry)	• Madeira cake with buttercream filling • White chocolate chip cookies	• Shortcrust pastry apple tart • Lemon biscuits	• Melting point: Éclairs or profiteroles • Flash point: Searing steak	• Mayonnaise (used for prawn cocktail) • Vanilla ice cream

Possible Dishes

In this section, you must list possible dishes that illustrate the property/properties of a food, one of which must be your chosen dish. For example:

 Fats and oils have a wide variety of culinary uses, attributable to their properties, when used in food preparation. Prepare, make and serve one of the dishes you have investigated. (2010)

For this assignment, to demonstrate the properties of fats and oils, I could make a madeira cake with a buttercream filling (plasticity) **or** profiteroles (effects of heat).

Chosen Dish and Reasons for Choice

Go to page 46 of 'Common Topics in All Areas of Practice' for information on how to complete this section.

Sources of Information

Go to page 47 of 'Common Topics in All Areas of Practice' for information on how to complete this section.

Preparation and Planning (8 marks)

Go to page 47 of 'Common Topics in All Areas of Practice' for information on how to complete this section.

Implementation (28 marks)

Go to page 48 of 'Common Topics in All Areas of Practice' for information on how to complete this section.

Evaluation (12 marks)

Evaluation of Implementation

Go to page 51 of 'Common Topics in All Areas of Practice' for information on how to complete this section.

Evaluation of the Specific Requirements

In this section, you must evaluate your success in applying the property in question when making the selected dish, i.e. whether it was successful or unsuccessful.

The following example outlines the successful outcome of an assignment:

 Evaluate the assignment in terms of the success of the marinade in achieving its intended purpose.

My tandoori chicken marinade dish was successful:

When I cut the chicken it was soft and tender. I only needed to apply a little pressure and it simply flaked apart. This showed that my marinade was successful in tenderising the chicken, mainly due to the acidity of the natural yoghurt. By marinating it for a few hours, the yoghurt helped to tenderise the meat fibres, making it soft and easy to chew.

The tandoori marinade also gave the chicken a wonderful flavour. The chicken was infused with the flavour of onion, garlic and spices. I really enjoyed this dish and was amazed at the flavour of the chicken compared to the normal bland taste I am used to. Therefore, I can say with certainty that the marinade was successful.

The example below discusses the unsuccessful outcome of an assignment:

 Evaluate the assignment in terms of success in achieving the desired texture (aeration).

My pavlova dish was unsuccessful:

I whisked the eggs for the required length of time. However, they did not increase in size as I expected them to. I knew then that very little air had been incorporated. Although I did my best to follow all of the rules, my bowl could have been dirty or the eggs I used might have been too cold, as I forgot to take them out of the fridge beforehand. Even after all the whisking, the mixture was much smaller than the mixtures made by my classmates. Perhaps I over-whisked it? This could have resulted in a loss of volume.

When I took the pavlova out of the oven, it was very flat compared to the pavlovas made by my classmates. I did not achieve a marshmallow-soft centre, which was the desired texture. It all came down to the fact that I did not incorporate the amount of air necessary to achieve a light and airy pavlova. Overall, it was very disappointing. However, I have learned that, for this property to be successful, many rules need to be followed. I will take more care next time and hopefully it will be a success.

MY PERSONAL NOTES:
Area of Practice D: Properties of a Food

(Use this space to take notes during class or to record your personal research on Area of Practice D.)

Area of Practice E: Comparative Analysis including Sensory Analysis

One assignment **may** be issued in Area of Practice E. This will involve using a sensory analysis test to either:

- Compare two or more food products (e.g. different brands of crisps).

OR

- Carry out a sensory evaluation of a food (e.g. a nutritious breakfast cereal).

Key Requirements of Area of Practice E

If you choose an assignment from Area of Practice E, you may be expected to:

- Investigate and research the food products or dishes outlined in the assignment brief.
- Define the test outlined in the assignment, state the aim of the test and outline the possible outcomes.
- Explain how the test should be carried out.
- List the conditions to be controlled during testing.
- Choose examples of the food products/dishes you will test and give two reasons for your choice.
- Prepare, cook and evaluate your chosen dish.

These key requirements may differ depending on the assignment specifications. Make sure to read the assignment brief carefully and highlight the key requirements. This will help you to lay out all of the necessary points under the correct headings. We will now look at what should be included under each heading area for Area of Practice E.

Investigation: Analysis/Research (32 marks)

Analysis and Research

Begin the investigation by introducing the topic of sensory analysis. For example:

Sensory analysis is a scientific discipline used to measure, analyse and interpret reactions to the characteristics of food, as perceived by our senses of sight, sound, smell, taste and touch.

The layout of your investigation will depend on the key requirements of the assignment. For example:

 Investigate the different types of commercially prepared soups available (i.e. brands, flavours, methods of processing used). (2009)

An investigation of the range of commercially prepared soups available:

Brand	Flavour	Method of processing	Salt content per 100 g	Price
Cully & Sully 400 g tub	Chicken and vegetable soup	Fresh, refrigerated	0.9 g	€2.49
Knorr 60 g packet	Beef and vegetable soup	Dried	0.73 g	€1.27
Heinz 400 g tin	Vegetable soup	Canned	0.7 g	€1.35

(Please note that this is only a sample of what is required. Further detail is required for this answer.)

 Commercial soft drinks are very popular among young people. Carry out research on commercially available soft drinks that are popular with teenagers. Include reference to brands, flavours, price, sizes, packaging etc. (2010)

Brand	Flavour	Price	Size	Packaging
Club Orange (Britvic Ireland Ltd)	Orange	€1.29	500 ml	Plastic (recyclable)
Fanta (Coca-Cola HBC)	Orange	€1.35	500 ml	Plastic (recyclable)
Coca-Cola (Coca-Cola HBC)	Cola	€1.35	500 ml	Plastic (recyclable)
7Up (Britvic Ireland Ltd)	Lemon and lime	€1.29	500 ml	Plastic (recyclable)

(Please note that this is only a sample of what is required. Further detail is required for this answer.)

When defining the test specified in the assignment brief, you must:

- Describe the test and provide a detailed account of how it should be carried out.
- Explain the purpose or aim of the test.
- Discuss the possible outcomes of the test.

For example:

 Using two different brands (one to be a supermarket's own brand) of fruit juice with the same flavour and texture, carry out a triangle test to determine if tasters can differentiate between the branded and non-branded juice. (2007)

Triangle test: fruit juice	
Description	The tester is presented with three coded samples of fruit juice. Two of the samples are the same and one is different. The tester is asked to identify the sample that is different.
Aim of test	To find out if there is a detectable difference.
Possible outcomes	There is a noticeable difference between products.

How to carry out a triangle test:

- Code 18 containers:
  - 6 containers with symbol ☐
  - 6 containers with symbol ◇
  - 6 containers with symbol ○.
- Put product samples in each container.
- Set up 6 trays numbered 1 to 6.
- Each tray should have one container labelled with symbol ☐, one container with symbol ◇, one container with symbol ○.

(Please note that this is only a sample of what is required. Further detail is required for this answer.)

The conditions required for testing must then be clearly explained. For example:

- Ensure adequate space between testers. This is to prevent the sharing of information, which could unfairly influence testers, resulting in inaccurate results.
- Correct lighting is essential when testing, as a dark room might affect the colour of the food or hide imperfections. Desks should be moved to a window in order to view the food in natural light.

(Please note that this is only a sample of what is required. Further detail is required for this answer.)

Possible Food Products/Dishes

In this section, you must list the possible dishes or food products that meet the key requirements of the assignment. For example:

 Commercial soft drinks are very popular among young people. Using two different brands of soft drink, both with the same flavour, carry out a Difference test. (2010)

For this assignment I could choose Club Orange (Britvic Ireland Ltd) and Fanta (Coca-Cola HBC) OR Coca-Cola (Coca-Cola HBC) and Tesco Cola (Tesco Stores Ltd).

Chosen Products/Dishes and Reasons for Choice

Go to page 46 of 'Common Topics in All Areas of Practice' for information on how to complete this section.

Sources of Information

Go to page 47 of 'Common Topics in All Areas of Practice' for information on how to complete this section.

Preparation and Planning (8 marks)

In this section you must:

- List the products to be tested and their cost. For example:

 Commercial pizzas are very popular due to their convenience and the wide range available. Using two different brands of pizzas with similar toppings, carry out a descriptive rating test. (2006)

Tesco Everyday Value Pepperoni Pizza: €1.90

Dr. Oetker Ristorante Pepperoni Pizza: €3.99

If the assignment brief requires you to make the product for testing (e.g. scones), see page 47 for guidelines on how to list and cost ingredients.

- List the equipment required to carry out the test. For example:

 Many food companies offer a healthy option alternative to their products in order to improve their marketability e.g. low fat, low sugar, low salt. Carry out a triangle test to determine if tasters can differentiate between the original product and the healthy option alternative. (2013)

Key Equipment for a Triangle Test		
6 trays	6 glasses of water	18 coded containers
9 samples of Tesco Finest strawberry and cream yoghurt		
9 samples of Tesco low-fat strawberry yoghurt		
6 scorecards	1 record sheet	1 pen

 Salted crisps are a predominant part of the snack food market. Purchase two different brands of salted crisps. The crisps should be the same variety/type and flavour but contain different amounts of salt. Using a directional paired comparison test, compare the crisps in terms of saltiness. (2012)

Key Equipment for a Directional Paired Comparison Test		
6 trays	6 glasses of water	12 coded containers
6 samples of Tayto Cheese & Onion crisps		
6 samples of King Cheese & Onion crisps		
6 scorecards	1 record sheet	1 pen

If the assignment brief requires to make the dish/food product (e.g. a nutritious breakfast cereal), the equipment required to make the dish/product must also be listed. See page 47 for guidelines.

Implementation (28 marks)

In the Implementation section you must:

- Document all steps involved in the method/procedure when carrying out the test.
- State the results obtained and present these using a pie chart, bar chart or star diagram.
- Outline two key factors that apply to this test and state the reasons why they are important.
- Explain one hygiene point and one safety point that should be adhered to and explain why.

Method/Procedure

If the assignment brief requires you to make a dish/product (e.g. scones), you should refer to page 48 for guidelines on how to describe the implementation. You should then continue with the method/procedure for how to carry out the test.

When explaining the method/procedure, you must write a detailed step-by-step description of how the test outlined in the assignment was carried out. For example:

 The variety and quality of commercially prepared soups are constantly being extended and improved. Prepare three convenience soups. (Soups should be the same flavour, but different brands or manufactured using a different method of processing.) Using a descriptive ranking test, compare the soups in terms of saltiness. (2009)

A Descriptive Ranking Test of Soups:

- I prepared myself by tying back my hair, putting on my apron and washing my hands, ensuring that I adhered to best hygiene practices.
- I then prepared my work station by gathering all essential equipment from my equipment list.
- I poured the fresh carton soup into a saucepan and heated on a medium heat for 5 minutes.
- I put the dried packet of soup in a saucepan, added 400 ml of cold water and stirred them together to dissolve. I brought it to the boil and then reduced it to a simmer for 4 minutes.
- Finally, I opened the can of soup, poured it into another saucepan and added two cans of water. I brought it to the boil and then reduced to a simmer for 4 minutes.

Test:

- We decided which symbol represented each soup sample:
    - □ = Campbell's canned soup
    - ○ = Erin dried soup
    - ◊ = Avonmore fresh carton soup.
- We coded the containers with the three different symbols (□, ○ and ◊).
- We labelled the scorecards and added clear instructions for the testers and typed out our record sheet to record results.
- We set up the six trays, each with three spoons, a glass of water, a pen and a scorecard.

(Please note that this is only a sample of what is required. Further detail is required for this answer.)

Results:

Once the test is complete, calculate the results obtained and present them using a pie chart, bar chart or star diagram. The type of chart you use will depend on the test outlined in the assignment.

For example:

- 80% of testers thought Erin dried soup was the saltiest.
- 15% thought that Campbell's tinned soup was the saltiest.
- 5% thought Avonmore fresh carton soup was the saltiest.

Therefore, according to our research, Erin dried soup is the saltiest commercial soup.

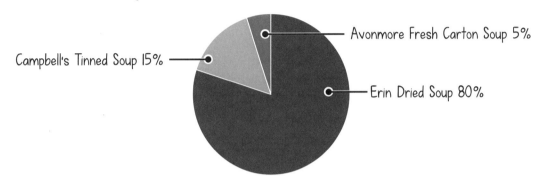

Avonmore Fresh Carton Soup 5%

Campbell's Tinned Soup 15%

Erin Dried Soup 80%

(Please note that this is only a sample of what is required. Further detail is required for this answer.)

If the assignment is a Descriptive Rating Test, you will be asked to present your findings on a star diagram or line chart. For example:

 Design and produce a simple product suitable for selling at a local country/food market. Make the product. Carry out a descriptive rating test using line scales or star diagrams. (Use 6 attributes.) Compile a sensory profile of the product made. (2016)

How to create a star diagram:

1. Decide on the characteristics/attributes you are going to include in your star diagram. This will help form the product specification indicating how the product should look and taste.
2. Draw a graph with lines radiating from a centre point to make a star. Each line represents one of the characteristics chosen.
3. Label each line with a characteristic/attribute (e.g. sweetness).
4. Mark each line with numbers from 1 to 5 (a 5-point hedonic scale).

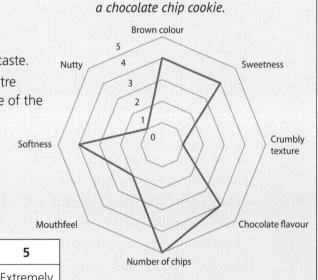

Results of a descriptive rating test on a chocolate chip cookie.

0	1	2	3	4	5
Not at all	A little	Somewhat	Fairly	Very	Extremely

5. Once the results have been collated, mark each characteristic/attribute on the chart.
6. Join each score marked.

Using the results obtained, compile a **sensory** profile. A sensory profile is a detailed description of the product. For example:

A sensory profile of chocolate chip cookies suitable for selling at a local country/food market:

These cookies are soft in texture with a lot of chocolate chips. They also have a rich brown colour and are very sweet. They are not crumbly biscuits and they do not have a very strong nutty flavour.

Key Factors

Go to page 50 of 'Common Topics in All Areas of Practice' for information on how to complete this section.

Safety

Go to page 51 of 'Common Topics in All Areas of Practice' for information on how to complete this section.

Hygiene

Go to page 51 of 'Common Topics in All Areas of Practice' for information on how to complete this section.

Evaluation (12 marks)

Evaluation of Implementation

In this section, you must evaluate and fully describe one or more of the following:
- The efficiency of the testing procedures used.
- The key factors you followed when conducting the test.
- The safety and hygiene issues you considered when conducting the test.
- The problems you encountered when conducting the test, and your suggested solutions.
- The efficiency of your work sequence.

The example below outlines how to evaluate the efficiency of the testing procedures used:

 Many food companies offer a healthy option alternative to their products in order to improve their marketability e.g. low fat, low sugar, low salt. Carry out a triangle test to determine if tasters can differentiate between the original product and the healthy option alternative. Evaluate the assignment in terms of implementation. (2013)

Before we started the test, we fully researched the conditions to be followed when testing, as well as the specific steps in setting up and carrying out the triangle test. This was hugely beneficial to us as we all knew what we were supposed to do, each group followed the steps and the test itself ran smoothly. The organisers set perfect trays and ensured the room was suitable for testing. The testers were fully aware of what was expected of them and carried out the tasting accurately. They didn't ask for the instructions to be repeated and they didn't look uncertain of what they were doing at any stage. We knew the test had been implemented successfully when the score cards were collected and were filled in correctly. I am happy to say that the test was implemented successfully, mainly due to our prior knowledge and thorough preparation.

Evaluation of the Specific Requirements:

In this section, you must:

- Analyse the test results obtained and outline the factors that may have contributed to these results.

OR

- If a descriptive ranking test was completed, you will be asked to evaluate how the product made compares to the product specification.

The following example shows how to analyse the test results:

BRIEF

Using three different brands of milk chocolate, carry out a preference ranking test to determine which brand of chocolate is the preferred choice within your group. Evaluate the assignment in terms of the test results obtained (i.e. an analysis of the factors that may contribute to the test results obtained). (2014)

Our results show that 65% of testers preferred Green & Black's milk chocolate, 25% preferred Tesco milk chocolate and 10% preferred Galaxy milk chocolate. Therefore, we can say that Green & Black's is the preferred chocolate. This could be because Green & Black's had the highest cocoa solids content at 37%. Whereas Tesco milk chocolate contained 27% cocoa solids and Galaxy contained only 25% cocoa solids. The percentage of cocoa solids obviously has an impact on the flavour of the chocolate. I was surprised by the result because I expected Galaxy to be in first place, as it is a popular bar in our school. I did not expect Tesco to come in second place, but the testers enjoyed it. This shows how a preconceived idea could influence results. By removing the wrappers we were able to judge the different types of chocolate without knowing what brands they were. This was an interesting sensory analysis test.

The example below shows how to evaluate how the product made compares to the product specification:

BRIEF

Design and produce a nutritious breakfast cereal as part of a school's healthy eating campaign. The cereal should appeal to teenagers. Your group should choose one product to develop and give reasons for the group's choice. Compile a product specification for the breakfast cereal (appearance, taste, etc.) using 6 attributes. Evaluate the assignment in terms of how the product made compares with the product specification. (2011)

Our product specification stated that our cereal should have been sweet, fruity, crunchy, nutty and attractive to look at. However, when we collated our results we found that the testers said it was not very sweet (Score 1), it did not look attractive (Score 2) and the flavour was too nutty (Score 5). Therefore, to modify the recipe I would:

- Add 30 ml of honey to add a natural sweetness
- Add dried cranberries to make it look more colourful and attractive
- Reduce the quantity of nuts by 40 g.

With these modifications I feel it would be a cereal that would appeal to more testers.

MY PERSONAL NOTES:
Area of Practice E: Comparative Analysis including Sensory Analysis

(Use this space to take notes during class or to record your personal research on Area of Practice E.)

_____

_____

_____

_____

_____

_____

_____

_____

_____

_____

_____

_____

_____

_____

_____

_____

_____

_____

_____

_____

_____

_____

_____

_____

_____

_____

_____

_____

_____

_____

_____

COMMON TOPICS IN ALL AREAS OF PRACTICE

Certain recording criteria are **common** to all five assignments in the Food Studies Practical Coursework Journal:

1. **Investigation: Analysis/Research:**
   - Chosen Dish/Food Product(s) and Reasons for Choice
   - Sources of Information

2. **Preparation and Planning:**
   - Key Equipment
   - Ingredients
   - Cost of Each Ingredient and the Total Cost of the Dish

3. **Implementation:**
   - Method/Procedure
   - Key Factors
   - Safety
   - Hygiene

4. **Evaluation:**
   - Evaluation of Implementation

Investigation

Chosen Dish/Food Product(s) and Reasons for Choice

In this section, you must choose a dish/food product(s) that meets the requirements of the assignment. The dish/food product(s) must be clearly named using the heading 'My chosen dish/food product(s)'.

Give two well-developed reasons why you chose the dish/food product(s). Reasons should relate to the research you have carried out.

The following example is for Area of Practice A:

 As people grow older, it is important that their changing dietary and nutritional needs are considered when planning meals. Prepare, cook and serve <u>one</u> of the main courses that you have investigated. (2012)

My chosen dish: Homemade fish pie topped with mashed potatoes, served with steamed carrots and spinach.

Reasons for choice:

Reason 1: I chose fish pie as it is a nutritionally balanced meal for an older person. The dish includes foods from all four food groups. Potatoes (from the bread, cereals and potatoes group) contain carbohydrates. Peas, carrots and spinach (from the fruit and vegetables group) provide vitamins A and C and minerals (iron). Fish (from the protein group) is an easily digestible source of high biological value protein. The white sauce contains milk and the pie is topped with cheese. These contain calcium.

Reason 2: Fish pie is also suitable for an older person as it is soft and easy to chew. This is especially important for those with dentures or people who may have difficulty handling cutlery due to arthritis. The soft fish and white sauce means that this dish is easier for an older person to digest. It will not cause discomfort or heartburn.

The example below is for Area of Practice D:

 The success of many dishes relies on the gelatinisation of starch which may be present in one or more ingredients. Prepare, cook and serve one of the dishes (either sweet or savoury) that you have investigated. (2015)

My chosen dish: Lemon meringue pie

Reasons for choice:

Reason 1: I chose lemon meringue pie because gelatinisation occurs in the lemon curd. When heated, the starch cells in the cornflour swell, burst and absorb the lemon juice. This causes the mixture to thicken and gelatinise to form a set curd that can be poured over the pastry base.

Reason 2: Gelatinisation also occurs in the pastry base of a lemon meringue pie. When the pastry is baked in a hot oven, the starch cells in the flour swell, burst and absorb the melted fat. This results in a short, crumbly-textured pastry, which contrasts nicely with the lemon curd and meringue.

Sources of Information

You will need to name **two** sources of information that were used for your research. Give full details of each source.

If you are listing a book, make sure to give the complete book title and the author's name(s). For example:

Source 1: 'Complete Home Economics' by Leanne Gillick and Laura Healy.

If you are listing a website, give the complete website address. For example:

Source 2: www.bordbia.ie or http://www.hse.ie/eng/health/az/.

Preparation and Planning

In this section in Areas of Practice A, B, C and D, you are expected to give a detailed list of:

- The ingredients used in the making your chosen dish/food product.
- The cost of each ingredient and the total cost of the dish/food product.
- The key equipment used in the making of your chosen dish/food product.

Ingredients

- If your chosen dish/food product has many components, use sub-headings when you are listing the ingredients (e.g. for lemon meringue pie use 'Pastry', 'Filling' and 'Meringue').
- When stating the quantities of ingredients, ensure that they are accurate. Use the correct units of measurement (e.g. 100 g of flour, 50 ml of milk).
- Ensure costings are included for each ingredient (see below for how to calculate this) and that they are within a realistic price range. Include the total cost of all ingredients at the end.

Cost of Each Ingredient and the Total Cost of the Dish/Food Product

How to calculate the cost of the quantity of ingredients used:

Total cost ÷ total weight (in g/ml) = cost of 1 g/ml × weight used (in g/ml) = cost of amount used.

Here is an example:

If 2 kg (2000 g) of plain flour costs €2.99, how much is 150 g of plain flour?

1. Divide the total cost by the total weight (in grams) of the product:

$$\frac{€2.99}{2000\ g} = €0.001495$$

This gives you the price of 1 g of the product.

2. Then multiply the price of 1 g by the quantity (in grams) used:

$$€0.001495 × 150\ g = €0.22$$

Therefore, 150 g of plain flour = **22 cents**.

You may find the following websites useful when you are costing your ingredients:

- www.tesco.ie (click on 'Shop Online – Get Started')
- www.supervalu.ie (click on 'Shop').

Key Equipment

- When listing the equipment needed for your chosen dish/food product, make sure to include all items including any specialised equipment (e.g. ice-cream maker).
- Always include a serving dish/container for serving the dish/food product at the end.

The following example shows you how to list ingredients and key equipment:

Chicken and Vegetable Stir-Fry with Wholegrain Rice

Ingredient/ Product	Cost	Ingredient/Product	Cost	Key Equipment/ Testing Equipment
3 chicken fillets	€3.99	1 thumb-sized piece of fresh ginger	35 cent	2 chopping boards
1 onion	21 cent	1 teaspoon of Chinese five-spice powder	5 cent	2 sharp knives
1 red pepper	79 cent	A pinch of salt	1 cent	Vegetable peeler
1 green pepper	79 cent	1 tablespoon of cornflour	10 cent	Garlic crusher
6 baby corn	82 cent	A sprig of parsley (to garnish)	3 cent	Grater
1 carrot	22 cent			Wooden spoon
200 g of wholegrain rice	36 cent			Measuring spoons
1 tablespoon of olive oil	15 cent			Colander
2 tablespoons of soy sauce	32 cent			Wok
1 fresh green chilli	38 cent			Containers for prepared ingredients
2 cloves of garlic	30 cent			Pot stand
		Total	€8.87	Serving plate

Implementation

Method/Procedure

In this section you must write a detailed step-by-step description of how the chosen dish/food product was made. (You can write the description in the past or present tense.) Please note the following guidelines:

- Each assignment should be written using numbers or bullet points to make it easier for the examiner to read and mark.
- It should include:
  - A description of how you prepared yourself and your work station.
  - A detailed description of the steps you followed when preparing and cooking your dish/food product.
  - A description of how you served the dish/food product.
  - Reference to the cleaning of your work station and evaluation of your dish under the headings given.
- Make sure you do not leave out any stages (e.g. 'I drained the rice using a colander.').
- Document the method in a logical sequence (e.g. 'I baked the pastry blind before adding the filling.').
- Always explain how each ingredient was prepared in detail (e.g. 'I topped and tailed the carrot, peeled it to remove the skin and cut it into thin julienne strips.').
- Be sure to include the temperatures used to cook the food and the length of time taken for each step (e.g. 'I stir-fried the carrot strips on a high heat for 4 minutes.' or 'I baked the dish in a hot oven at 200 °C for 20 minutes.').
- Describe how you served the dish (e.g. 'I served a slice of lemon meringue pie with a swirl of whipped cream and a sprig of mint as a garnish.').

N.B. The method should **not** be directly transcribed from the recipe book. It should be an account of how you made the dish, written in your **own words.**

The examples below show you how to write the method/procedure.

The following example is for Area of Practice A:

 Many third-level students living away from home find shopping and cooking for themselves a new and challenging experience. Prepare, cook and serve one of the main courses from your research. (2015)

Chicken and Vegetable Stir-Fry with Wholegrain Rice:

- I prepared myself by tying back my hair, putting on my apron and washing my hands. I then prepared my work area by gathering all of the equipment from my equipment list and weighing my ingredients.
- On a chopping board, I trimmed any fat or unwanted parts from my chicken fillets. I sliced each fillet into even-sized thin strips using a sharp knife. I put them in a bowl in the fridge until I was ready to begin.
- I rinsed the peppers, baby corn and chilli under running water to remove any chemical residue or dirt.
- I used a separate chopping board and knife to prepare the vegetables. I began by removing the end of the garlic clove and peeling it. I crushed the clove with the back of my knife and then chopped it finely.

(Please note that this is only a sample of what is required. Further detail is required for this answer.)

The example below is for Area of Practice C:

BRIEF **The popularity of 'Afternoon Tea' has led to an increasing interest in home baking. Using one of the techniques/methods investigated, prepare and bake one product suitable for serving at afternoon tea. (2016)**

Cranberry and Orange Scones with Orange Butter

- I prepared myself by tying back my hair, putting on my apron and washing my hands. I then prepared my work area by gathering all of the equipment from my equipment list and weighing my ingredients.
- I preheated the oven to 200 °C/180 °C fan/gas mark 6.
- I lightly dusted two baking trays with flour. This was to prevent the scones from sticking to the tray.
- I washed the orange. I removed the zest using the fine side of a grater.
- I sieved the flour into a large mixing bowl. I added a pinch of salt, the baking powder and the caster sugar.
- I cut the butter into small cubes, then using my fingertips I rubbed it into the flour, salt, baking powder and caster sugar until it resembled coarse breadcrumbs.

(Please note that this is only a sample of what is required. Further detail is required for this answer.)

Key Factors

A key factor is an essential step that is critical to the success of your chosen dish. You must mention **two** key factors that apply to your chosen dish. You must fully explain **why** they are necessary.

N.B. Do not repeat the same key factors across the assignments.

The following examples show you how the key factors should be written.

The example below is for Area of Practice B:

BRIEF **The variety of yeast breads available to consumers has increased in recent years. Prepare, cook and serve one of the products from your research. (2010)**

Key Factor: I left my bread to prove for 1 hour in a warm place as this created a suitable environment for the yeast to work. Yeast needs time and warmth in order to produce carbon dioxide bubbles. The carbon dioxide bubbles allow the dough to double in size, producing a light, aerated bread. If I had not carried out the proving stage, the dough would have been flat. This would have affected the final texture of the bread, making it dense and heavy.

The following example is for Area of Practice D:

BRIEF **The success of many dishes relies on the gelatinisation of starch which may be present in one or more ingredients. Prepare, cook and serve one of the dishes (either sweet or savoury) that you have investigated. (2015)**

Key Factor: When making the white roux sauce I stirred the flour into the melted butter and put it back on the heat to cook for 1 minute. The heat caused the starch cells in the flour to expand and burst. When the milk was whisked in after, the starch cells absorbed the milk, resulting in the thickening of the sauce due to gelatinisation. Had I not heated the flour and butter, the sauce would not have thickened and would have tasted floury.

Safety

Each assignment requires you to mention **one** safety point that must specifically relate to an ingredient/step involved in your chosen dish/food product that could potentially cause injury or harm (e.g. cut, burn, scald, electric shock).

It is very important to fully explain the reason **why** this safety point is necessary.

The following examples will show you how the safety point should be written:

> **Safety:** When I was slicing the onion, I used a sharp knife because blunt knives are more likely to slip. I made sure to curl in my fingertips, which protected my fingers from being cut by the blade, thus preventing serious injury.

OR

> **Safety:** When removing my Mediterranean quiche from the oven, I made sure to use oven gloves as the oven was 200 °C and the dish could have caused serious burns to my hands if I had used a tea towel or dishcloth.

Hygiene

Each assignment requires you to mention **one** hygiene point that must specifically relate to an ingredient/step involved in making your chosen dish. The hygiene point could prevent food poisoning or a food-related illness.

It is very important to fully explain the reason **why** this hygiene point is necessary.

The following examples show you how the hygiene point should be written:

> **Hygiene:** When slicing the chicken fillets, I used a clean chopping board. I used a separate one for my vegetables (e.g. peppers) to prevent cross-contamination of salmonella bacteria from the raw chicken from occurring, as this could lead to serious food poisoning.

OR

> **Hygiene:** I cooked the minced meat on a high heat, stirring to ensure even cooking, until it was fully brown and no traces of pink remained. Otherwise bacteria (e.g. E.coli) may still have been present which could have caused food poisoning if consumed.

Evaluation

Evaluation of Implementation

This section is a critical analysis of your final dish. It can be answered under one or more of the following headings:

- A sensory review of the final dish or food product, taking into account appearance, colour, flavour and texture. Always refer to a specific ingredient or process that was key to the success or failure of the dish.
- Difficulties you encountered when you were making the final dish or food product and modifications you would recommend. Each modification must be linked to a difficulty that you have already mentioned.
- Skills you have used when making the final dish or food product and your efficient use of resources: time, ingredients, equipment and energy.

The following example shows you how to compile a sensory review of the final dish or food product:

Area of Practice D:

 Gelatine (gelatin) has a wide range of uses both culinary and in food manufacture. Prepare and make one of the dishes from your research. Evaluate the assignment in terms of implementation. (2014)

Pink Strawberry Cheesecake:

- **Appearance and colour:** The cheesecake looked very attractive. I used whole strawberries and white chocolate curls to decorate it. The cheesecake had set nicely on top of the biscuit base. The pieces of red strawberries contrasted with the creamy pink cheesecake filling. The biscuit provided a light brown layer at the base.

- **Flavour:** I enjoyed the sweet, fruity strawberry flavour of the cheesecake. The rich, creamy cheesecake filling worked well with the buttery biscuit base.

- **Texture:** I was relieved that the cheesecake had set adequately. When I cut into it, it held its shape, showing that the gelatine had set the liquid ingredients. However, when I removed the slice I found that the biscuit base crumbled apart and did not stay with the filling. This was disappointing and it affected the overall success of my cheesecake.

The example below shows you how to evaluate difficulties encountered when making the final dish or food product, and the modifications recommended:

Difficulty encountered and modification:

I was disappointed with the biscuit base in my cheesecake, as it broke when I cut a slice and lifted it away. It was also difficult to eat, as it kept crumbling. I think this occurred because there wasn't enough butter in the recipe to bind the biscuit crumbs together. Therefore, the next time I make this recipe I will add another 25 g of butter. This should prevent the base from falling apart. Also, using the food processor to crush the biscuits would result in finer crumbs, which would be more likely to stick together. When I crushed the biscuits by hand, the chunks were larger and fell out more easily. I have learned from this and now know how to rectify it in the future.

The example below shows you how to evaluate skills used when making the final dish or food product and the efficient use of resources:

Area of Practice C:

 The popularity of 'Afternoon Tea' has led to an increasing interest in home baking. Using one of the techniques/methods investigated, prepare and bake one product suitable for serving at afternoon tea. Evaluate the assignment in terms of implementation. (2016)

I chose to make lemon meringue pie as a product to be served for afternoon tea. I felt that it showed my skill progression from Junior Certificate, as it required that I make three separate parts for one dish. I had to make a rich shortcrust pastry, lemon curd and meringue. I carefully weighed my ingredients and organised them before starting to make sure I had everything to hand when needed. I made sure to follow the method carefully to ensure the success of the dish (e.g. a crumbly pastry, set curd and airy meringue). I also made sure to keep a close eye on the time to ensure that it was completed before the end of class. I had to work quickly and efficiently to achieve this. Overall the dish was a success, mainly due to my careful preparation and efficient work ethic.

FOOD STUDIES PRACTICAL COURSEWORK ASSIGNMENT TOPICS

The Food Studies Practical Coursework Assignment Topics that have appeared in Leaving Certificate Home Economics assignment briefs from 2004 to 2017 are listed in the tables below. The topics are listed under the relevant areas of practice. The marking schemes for each assignment brief are available on *www.examinations.ie*.

Area of Practice A – Application of Nutritional Principles

Year	Assignment 1	Assignment 2	
2017	Young children (2–5 years)	Iron deficiency anaemia	
2016	Young people who participate in active sport	Older person (loss of body weight and muscle mass)	
2015	Third-level students living in shared accommodation	High-salt diet	
2014	Family with a range of dietary needs and a limited budget	Poor cardiovascular health	
2013	School-going children (6–12 years)	Vegetarian	
2012	Older people	Childhood obesity (school-going children)	
2011	Family with young children (12–24 months)	Low Glycaemic Index (GI) diet	
2010	Low-income family	Osteoporosis (women 50 years+)	
2009	Young people who participate in active sport	Women (18–50 years) with inadequate iron intake	
2008	Family with young children (2–5 years)	Adults who are overweight or obese	
2007	School-going teenagers (12–18 years)	Low-sugar diet OR diabetic diet	
2006	Older people	High-salt diet	Childhood obesity
2005	Family with teenagers	Pregnancy (before and during)	High-fibre diet
2004	Low-income family (2 adults, 2 teenagers)	Lacto vegetarian or vegan	Coronary heart disease

Area of Practice B – Food Preparation and Cooking Processes

Year	Assignment 3
2017	Food safety
2016	Food processor
2015	Commercially prepared pastry
2014	Gelatine
2013	Rough puff/choux pastry
2012	Electric food mixer or hand blender
2011	Microwave oven

Year	Assignment 3
2010	Yeast bread
2009	Soufflé
2008	Wok or steamer
2007	Roasting
2006	Food processor
2005	Commercial filo or puff pastry
2004	Yeast

Area of Practice C – Food Technology

Year	Assignment 4
2017	Homemade ice cream
2016	Home baking – afternoon tea
2015	Homemade bread
2014	Homemade pickle
2013	Homemade preserves – jam/jelly/ marmalade
2012	Homemade chutney or relish
2011	Home baking – muffins or cupcakes

Year	Assignment 4
2010	Homemade mincemeat
2009	Homemade yoghurt
2008	Homemade sweets and chocolates
2007	Homemade chutney or relish
2006	Homemade ice cream
2005	Homemade biscuits
2004	Fruit preserves

Area of Practice D – Properties of a Food

Year	Assignment 5
2017	N/A
2016	Properties of sugar
2015	Gelatinisation of starch
2014	Protein denaturation
2013	Marinade
2012	Properties of eggs
2011	Aeration

Year	Assignment 5
2010	Properties of fats and oils
2009	Gelatinisation of starch
2008	Caramelisation or coagulation
2007	Marinating
2006	Properties of sugar
2005	Aeration
2004	Gelatinisation of starch

Area of Practice E – Comparative Analysis including Sensory Analysis

Year	Assignment 6
2017	Commercially prepared pizzas – **preference ranking test**
2016	Product for a local country/food market – **descriptive rating test**
2015	Baked products using different types of fat – **simple difference paired comparison test**
2014	Commercial milk chocolate bars – **preference ranking test**
2013	Original product and healthy option alternative – **triangle test**
2012	Salted crisps – **directional paired comparison test**
2011	Nutritious breakfast cereal – **descriptive rating test**
2010	Commercial soft drinks – **difference test**
2009	Commercially prepared soups – **descriptive ranking test**
2008	Healthy snack for a school canteen – **descriptive rating test**
2007	Commercial fruit juices – **triangle test**
2006	Commercially prepared pizzas – **descriptive rating test** <u>and</u> **preference test**
2005	Commercial fruit yoghurts – **descriptive test** <u>and</u> **preference test**
2004	Homemade scones – **triangle test** <u>and</u> **preference test**

Home Economics - Practical Food Studies Assignment
Eacnamaíocht Bhaile - Tasc Praiticiúil i Staidéar Bia

Area of Practice:
Réimse Cleachtais:

Assignment No.
Uimhir an Taisc

PPSN
USPP

Assignment
Tasc

Marks for Assignment
Marcanna don Tasc

		Mark *Marc*
Investigation: Analysis and Research *Fiosrúchán: Anailís/Taighde*		32
Practical Application: *Feidhmiú Praiticiúil:*	**Planning and Preparation** *Ulmhúchán agus Pleanáil*	8
	Implementation *Feidhmiú*	28
	Evaluation *Measúnúchán*	12

Investigation: Analysis/Research (32 marks)
Fiosrúchán: Anailís/Taighde (32 marc)

	OFFICIAL USE ONLY DON OIFIG AMHÁIN	
	1	2

Sources of Information | *Foinsí na Faisnéise*

Practical Application – Preparation and Planning (8 marks)
Feidhmiú Praiticiúil - Ulmhúchán agus Pleanáil (8 marc)

Name of dish / test I *Ainm na Méise/an Tástála*
Source of recipe I *Foinse an Oidis*
Date of practical I *Dáta an Phraiticiúil*

Ingredients / Product *Comhábhair / Tairge*	Cost *Costas*	Ingredients *Comhábhair*	Cost *Costas*	Key Equipment / Testing Equipment *Príomh Fhearas / Trealamh Tástáil*	OFFICIAL USE ONLY DON OIFIG AMHÁIN	
					1	2
	Total I *Iomlán*					

Implementation (28 marks)
Feidhmiú (28 marc)

(to include procedure followed, key factors considered, safety and hygiene factors)
(an nós imeachta a leanadh, na príomhthosca a cuireadh san áireamh, tosca sábháilteacht agus sláinteachas san áireamh)

	1	2

Evaluation (12 marks)
Measúnúchán (12 marc)

(to include evaluation of implementation and specific requirements of the assignment)
(measúnúchán feidhmiú agus measúnúchán riachtanais shainiúla an tasc san áireamh)

	OFFICIAL USE ONLY DON OIFIG AMHÁIN	
	1	2

Home Economics - Practical Food Studies Assignment
Eacnamaíocht Bhaile - Tasc Praiticiúil i Staidéar Bia

Area of Practice:
Réimse Cleachtais:

Assignment No.
Uimhir an Taisc

PPSN
USPP

Assignment
Tasc

Marks for Assignment
Marcanna don Tasc

	Mark *Marc*
Investigation: Analysis and Research *Fiosrúchán: Anailís/Taighde*	32
Practical Application: *Feidhmiú Praiticiúil:*　　**Planning and Preparation** *Ulmhúchán agus Pleanáil*	8
Implementation *Feidhmiú*	28
Evaluation *Measúnúchán*	12

Investigation: Analysis/Research (32 marks)
Fiosrúchán: Anailís/Taighde (32 marc)

	OFFICIAL USE ONLY DON OIFIG AMHÁIN	
	1	2

Sources of Information | *Foinsí na Faisnéise*

Practical Application – Preparation and Planning (8 marks)
Feidhmiú Praiticiúil - Ulmhúchán agus Pleanáil (8 marc)

Name of dish / test I *Ainm na Méise/an Tástála*
Source of recipe I *Foinse an Oidis*
Date of practical I *Dáta an Phraiticiúil*

Ingredients / Product *Comhábhair / Tairge*	Cost *Costas*	Ingredients *Comhábhair*	Cost *Costas*	Key Equipment / Testing Equipment *Príomh Fhearas / Trealamh Tástáil*	OFFICIAL USE ONLY *DON OIFIG AMHÁIN* 1	2
	Total I *Iomlán*					

Implementation (28 marks)
Feidhmiú (28 marc)

(to include procedure followed, key factors considered, safety and hygiene factors)
(an nós imeachta a leanadh, na príomhthosca a cuireadh san áireamh, tosca sábháilteacht agus sláinteachas san áireamh)

	1	2

OFFICIAL USE ONLY DON OIFIG AMHÁIN	
1	2
1	2

Evaluation (12 marks)
Measúnúchán (12 marc)

(to include evaluation of implementation and specific requirements of the assignment)
(measúnúchán feidhmiú agus measúnúchán riachtanais shainiúla an tasc san áireamh)

	OFFICIAL USE ONLY DON OIFIG AMHÁIN	
	1	2

Home Economics - Practical Food Studies Assignment
Eacnamaíocht Bhaile - Tasc Praiticiúil i Staidéar Bia

Area of Practice:
Réimse Cleachtais:

Assignment No.
Uimhir an Taisc

PPSN
USPP

Assignment
Tasc

Marks for Assignment
Marcanna don Tasc

	Mark *Marc*
Investigation: Analysis and Research *Fiosrúchán: Anailís/Taighde*	32
Practical Application: *Feidhmiú Praiticiúil:* **Planning and Preparation** *Ulmhúchán agus Pleanáil*	8
Implementation *Feidhmiú*	28
Evaluation *Measúnúchán*	12

Investigation: Analysis/Research (32 marks)
Fiosrúchán: Anailís/Taighde (32 marc)

	OFFICIAL USE ONLY DON OIFIG AMHÁIN
	1	2

Sources of Information I *Foinsí na Faisnéise*

Practical Application – Preparation and Planning (8 marks)
Feidhmiú Praiticiúil - Ulmhúchán agus Pleanáil (8 marc)

Name of dish / test | *Ainm na Méise/an Tástála*

Source of recipe | *Foinse an Oidis*

Date of practical | *Dáta an Phraiticiúil*

Ingredients / Product *Comhábhair / Tairge*	Cost *Costas*	Ingredients *Comhábhair*	Cost *Costas*	Key Equipment / Testing Equipment *Príomh Fhearas / Trealamh Tástáil*	OFFICIAL USE ONLY DON OIFIG AMHÁIN	
					1	2
		Total | *Iomlán*				

Implementation (28 marks)
Feidhmiú (28 marc)

(to include procedure followed, key factors considered, safety and hygiene factors)
(an nós imeachta a leanadh, na príomhthosca a cuireadh san áireamh, tosca sábháilteacht agus sláinteachas san áireamh)

	1	2

72

OFFICIAL USE ONLY DON OIFIG AMHÁIN	
1	2
1	2

Evaluation (12 marks)
Measúnúchán (12 marc)

(to include evaluation of implementation and specific requirements of the assignment)
(measúnúchán feidhmiú agus measúnúchán riachtanais shainiúla an tasc san áireamh)

	OFFICIAL USE ONLY DON OIFIG AMHÁIN	
	1	2

Home Economics - Practical Food Studies Assignment
Eacnamaíocht Bhaile - Tasc Praiticiúil i Staidéar Bia

Area of Practice:
Réimse Cleachtais:

Assignment No.
Uimhir an Taisc

PPSN
USPP

Assignment
Tasc

Marks for Assignment
Marcanna don Tasc

		Mark *Marc*
Investigation: Analysis and Research *Fiosrúchán: Anailís/Taighde*		32
Practical Application: *Feidhmiú Praiticiúil:*	**Planning and Preparation** *Ulmhúchán agus Pleanáil*	8
	Implementation *Feidhmiú*	28
	Evaluation *Measúnúchán*	12

Investigation: Analysis/Research (32 marks)
Fiosrúchán: Anailís/Taighde (32 marc)

77

Sources of Information | *Foinsí na Faisnéise*

Practical Application – Preparation and Planning (8 marks)
Feidhmiú Praiticiúil - Ulmhúchán agus Pleanáil (8 marc)

Name of dish / test | *Ainm na Méise/an Tástála*
Source of recipe | *Foinse an Oidis*
Date of practical | *Dáta an Phraiticiúil*

Ingredients / Product *Comhábhair / Tairge*	Cost *Costas*	Ingredients *Comhábhair*	Cost *Costas*	Key Equipment / Testing Equipment *Príomh Fhearas / Trealamh Tástáil*	OFFICIAL USE ONLY DON OIFIG AMHÁIN	
					1	**2**
		Total | *Iomlán*				

Implementation (28 marks)
Feidhmiú (28 marc)

(to include procedure followed, key factors considered, safety and hygiene factors)
(an nós imeachta a leanadh, na príomhthosca a cuireadh san áireamh, tosca sábháilteacht agus sláinteachas san áireamh)

	1	2

	OFFICIAL USE ONLY DON OIFIG AMHÁIN	
	1	2
	79	

Evaluation (12 marks)
Measúnúchán (12 marc)

(to include evaluation of implementation and specific requirements of the assignment)
(measúnúchán feidhmiú agus measúnúchán riachtanais shainiúla an tasc san áireamh)

	OFFICIAL USE ONLY DON OIFIG AMHÁIN	
	1	**2**

RECIPES

SAVOURY DISHES

DESSERTS AND CAKES

BREAD

PRESERVES

Butternut Squash and Coconut Soup

SUGGESTED AREAS OF PRACTICE

Area of Practice B: Food Preparation and Cooking Processes | Hand Blender

Serves: 4

Preparation Time: 20 minutes

Cooking Time: 15–20 minutes

Ingredients:

- 1 butternut squash
- 2 onions
- 3 cloves of garlic
- 1 red chilli
- 1 × 2½ cm piece of fresh ginger
- 1 tablespoon of peanut or sesame oil
- 50 g of butter
- 300 ml of water
- 1 chicken stock cube
- 1 × 400 ml can of coconut milk
- A pinch of salt and pepper

To garnish:
- 4 fresh coriander leaves

Method:

1. Remove the top and bottom of the butternut squash and remove the skin with a vegetable peeler. Cut the squash in half lengthwise, scoop out the seeds with a large spoon and chop into 2 cm cubes.

2. Top and tail the onion, remove the skin and dice finely.

3. Peel and finely chop or crush the garlic.

4. Remove the stalk of the chilli. Cut the chilli lengthwise, remove the seeds and membrane, and dice finely.

5. Peel the ginger and grate it, using the fine side of the grater.

6. Preheat a saucepan over a medium heat for 1 minute. Add the oil and butter.

7. When the butter has melted, add the butternut squash chunks, diced onion and garlic, and sauté for 5 minutes, stirring occasionally.

8. Add the diced chilli and grated ginger and cook for 3 minutes.

9. Boil the water in a kettle and pour it over the stock cube in a jug to dissolve it, whisking with a fork.

10. Add the hot stock and coconut milk to the saucepan.

11. Turn the heat up to high and bring the mixture to the boil. Reduce to a medium heat and simmer for 15–20 minutes or until the butternut squash is soft.

12. When cooked, remove the saucepan from the heat and allow the contents to cool for 5 minutes.

13. Using a hand blender, thoroughly blend the soup until smooth. Season with salt and pepper to taste.

14. Rinse the coriander leaves. Ladle a portion of the soup into a bowl. Garnish with a coriander leaf and serve.

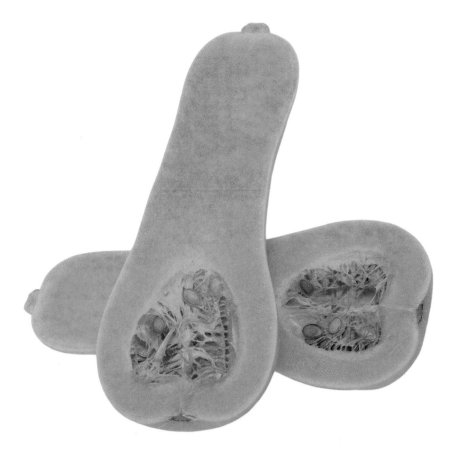

BUTTERNUT SQUASH AND COCONUT SOUP

Colcannon Soup with Parsley Pesto

(from *Clodagh's Irish Kitchen* by Clodagh McKenna)

SUGGESTED AREAS OF PRACTICE

Area of Practice B: Food Preparation and Cooking Processes | Blender/Hand Blender

Serves: 6

Preparation Time: 25 minutes

Cooking Time: 30 minutes

Ingredients:

- 50 g butter
- 300 g potatoes, peeled and diced
- 1 onion, diced
- 2 garlic cloves, crushed
- ½ teaspoon freshly grated nutmeg
- 800 ml hot chicken or vegetable stock
- 400g cabbage, sliced
- 200 ml single cream
- Sea salt and freshly ground black pepper

For the parsley pesto:

- 110 g fresh flat-leaf parsley
- 150 ml extra virgin olive oil
- 25 g pine kernels, toasted
- 1 garlic clove, crushed
- 50 g freshly grated Parmesan cheese

This recipe will need to be written into your *Food Studies Practical Coursework Journal* using the detailed recipe format found in the other recipes in this book.

This soup reinterprets the Irish classic 'colcannon', a dish that is made of mashed potatoes and kale or cabbage. You could add some pulled pork or pancetta to this soup if you wish.

Method:

1. Melt the butter in a heavy-bottomed saucepan over a medium heat. Add the potatoes, onion, garlic and nutmeg. Stir, cover, and reduce the heat to low. Leave to sweat for about 15 minutes, stirring occasionally.

2. Add the stock and bring the heat up to high. Let the onion and potatoes cook in the stock until they are completely soft, then add the cabbage – the cabbage will take only 5 minutes to cook.

3. While the cabbage is cooking, place all the ingredients for the parsley pesto in a food processor and blend until you have a smooth consistency. Set aside.

4. When the cabbage has wilted, stir in the cream, then pour the soup into a blender and whiz to a smooth consistency. Season with salt and pepper. Return to the pan to warm through if required.

5. To serve, pour the soup into warmed bowls and garnish with a generous drizzle of parsley pesto.

COLCANNON SOUP WITH PARSLEY PESTO

Mac 'n' Cheese

SUGGESTED AREAS OF PRACTICE

Area of Practice A: Application of Nutritional Principles | Toddlers/Children, Teenagers, Third-Level Students, Low-Salt Diet, Low-Income Family, Pregnancy, Osteoporosis, Older People

Area of Practice D: Properties of a Food | Properties of Starch: Gelatinisation

Serves: 4

Preparation Time: 20–25 minutes

Cooking Time: 20–25 minutes

Ingredients:

- 2 teaspoons of butter (for greasing)
- 1 medium cauliflower
- 1 onion
- 2 chicken fillets
- 150 g of white Cheddar cheese
- 250 g of macaroni
- 1 tablespoon of olive oil
- 50 g of butter
- 50 g of plain flour
- 800 ml of milk
- 1 teaspoon of wholegrain mustard
- A pinch of salt and pepper

For the topping:
- 50 g of white Cheddar cheese

To garnish:
- A sprig of parsley

TIP If you are cooking for toddlers or children, or for individuals trying to reduce their salt intake, omit the salt.

Method:

1. Preheat the oven to 200 °C/180 °C fan/gas mark 6.
   Grease the sides and base of a 25 cm × 25 cm ovenproof dish with the 2 teaspoons of butter.

2. Wash the cauliflower and divide into bite-size florets, using a knife.

3. Top and tail the onion, remove the skin and dice finely.

4. On a separate chopping board, trim any unwanted pieces from the chicken fillets and then cut into small bite-size chunks.

5. Grate the Cheddar cheese using the fine side of the grater and divide it into 150 g for the sauce and 50 g for the topping.

6. Boil a full kettle. Pour the boiling water into a large saucepan. Place the saucepan on a high heat. Carefully add the macaroni to the boiling water. Cook for 8 minutes. Stir the macaroni from time to time to stop it from sticking together. (You should also check the packet for instructions on cooking times.)

7. After the macaroni has been boiling for 4 minutes, add the cauliflower florets to the macaroni. Cook for 4 more minutes.

8. Drain the macaroni and cauliflower in a colander. Place them back in the saucepan and set them aside until later.

9. Preheat a frying pan for 1 minute over a high heat and add the olive oil. Add the chicken and cook for 6–7 minutes or until white/golden brown in colour. Lift the chicken out of the frying pan with a fish slice and place it on kitchen paper on a plate to remove excess oil.

 TIP If you do not have a 25 cm × 25 cm dish, something similar will do. Just make sure it is ovenproof.

Cheese roux sauce:

10. Heat a medium-sized saucepan over a medium heat for 1 minute. Add the butter. When the butter has melted, add the onion and sauté for 3–4 minutes or until the onions are translucent and soft.

11. Add the flour and stir until combined. Cook for 1 minute, stirring all the time, before removing the saucepan from the heat.

12. Add the milk little by little, stirring well each time with a whisk. Continue until all the liquid has been incorporated.

13. Place the saucepan back on the heat and cook for 3–4 minutes or until the sauce has thickened, stirring all the time.

14. Add the grated cheese and the wholegrain mustard. Stir through until the cheese has melted. Remove the saucepan from the heat.

Assembly:

15. Pour the cheese sauce into the saucepan with the macaroni and cauliflower and mix through until everything is combined. Add the chicken and mix through. Season with salt and pepper to taste.

16. Pour the contents of the saucepan into the ovenproof dish and sprinkle with the remaining cheese.

17. Bake in the oven for 20–25 minutes or until the top has turned golden and the sauce is bubbling up the sides. Remove the dish from the oven and allow it to cool slightly.

18. Garnish with a sprig of parsley and serve.

MAC 'N' CHEESE

Spaghetti and Meatballs in a Tomato and Basil Sauce

SUGGESTED AREAS OF PRACTICE

Area of Practice A: Application of Nutritional Principles | Toddlers/Children, Teenagers, Third-Level Students, Low-Salt Diet, Low-Income Family, Active Young Person, Pregnancy, Older People, Anaemia

Area of Practice B: Food Preparation and Cooking Processes | Food Safety

Serves: 4   **Preparation Time:** 35 minutes   **Cooking Time:** 15 minutes

Ingredients:

For the meatballs:

- ½ a red onion
- 1 clove of garlic
- 400 g of lean beef mince
- 100 g of sausage meat
- 100 g of breadcrumbs
- 1 teaspoon of Dijon mustard
- 2 tablespoons of tomato ketchup
- 1 teaspoon of dried oregano
- A pinch of salt and pepper
- 1 egg

For the sauce:

- 1 clove of garlic
- 1 tablespoon of olive oil
- ½ a red onion
- 1 × 400 g tin of chopped tomatoes
- 1 × 500 ml carton of passata
- 1 tablespoon of tomato purée
- 1 teaspoon of caster sugar
- A pinch of salt and pepper
- 8 fresh basil leaves

To serve:

- 300 g of wholemeal spaghetti
- 25 g of Parmesan or Cheddar cheese

To garnish:

- 4 fresh basil leaves

 TIP If you are making this dish for toddlers or children, vegetables can be 'hidden' in the tomato sauce. Finely grate a carrot and courgette into the onion and garlic before adding the tinned tomatoes.

Method:

Meatballs:

1. Top and tail the red onion, remove the skin and dice finely. Use half of the diced onions for the meatballs and set aside half for the tomato sauce.
2. Peel and finely chop or crush the garlic.
3. Place the mince, sausage meat, breadcrumbs, onion and garlic in a large bowl.
4. Add the mustard, ketchup, oregano and a pinch of salt and pepper.
5. Beat the egg in a bowl and add to the mixture.
6. Thoroughly mix everything together to form a large ball.
7. Remove a teaspoonful of the mixture and roll it into a small ball, using wet hands. Place on a large baking tray or plate. Work through all of the mixture in the same way.
8. Cover with cling film and chill the meatballs in the fridge to firm up.

Tomato sauce:

9. Peel and finely chop or crush the garlic clove.
10. Preheat a large saucepan over a medium heat for 1 minute and add the olive oil.
11. Sauté the onion for 3 minutes or until it is translucent and soft, then add the garlic and cook for 1 minute.
12. Add the tinned tomatoes, passata, tomato purée and sugar. Turn the heat up to high and bring the mixture to the boil. Reduce to a medium heat and simmer for 15–20 minutes or until the sauce has thickened.
13. Season to taste with a pinch of salt and pepper.
14. Rinse the basil leaves. Layer them on top of each other and roll them up tightly, then chop them using a sharp knife. Stir them into the sauce.

 If you are cooking this for toddlers or children, or individuals trying to lower their salt intake, omit the salt.

Spaghetti:

15. Boil a full kettle. Pour the boiling water into a large saucepan. Place the saucepan on a high heat. Carefully add the spaghetti to the boiling water. Cook for 8–10 minutes or until al dente (fully cooked, but still firm). Stir the spaghetti from time to time to stop it from sticking together. (You should also check the packet for instructions on cooking times.)

 You can add a teaspoon of olive oil to the spaghetti to prevent it from sticking together.

Final stage:

16. Remove the meatballs from the fridge and add them to the saucepan with the sauce. Gently stir in the meatballs until they are completely covered with sauce, being careful not to break them up.
17. Turn the heat back up to high to bring the sauce to the boil again, then reduce to a medium heat and simmer for a further 10–15 minutes, until the sauce has thickened.
18. Remove the sauce from the heat.
19. Grate the Parmesan or Cheddar cheese.
20. Drain the spaghetti using a colander.
21. On a serving plate, place the meatballs and sauce on a bed of spaghetti. Garnish with the grated cheese and a fresh basil leaf and serve.

SPAGHETTI AND MEATBALLS IN A TOMATO AND BASIL SAUCE

Hake, Leek and Asparagus Risotto

SUGGESTED AREAS OF PRACTICE

Area of Practice A: Application of Nutritional Principles | Toddlers/Children, Teenagers, Pregnancy, Coronary Heart Disease, Low-Salt Diet, Older People

Serves: 4

Preparation Time: 20 minutes

Cooking Time: 40 minutes

Ingredients:

- 700 g of hake fillets
- 1 leek
- 200 g of asparagus
- 1 clove of garlic
- 700 ml of water
- 1 fish or vegetable stock cube
- 200 ml of milk
- 1 tablespoon of olive oil
- 20 g (a small knob) of butter
- 300 g of Carnaroli or Arborio risotto rice
- A pinch of salt and pepper
- 50 g of frozen peas
- 3 tablespoons of crème fraîche
- 50 g of Parmesan cheese

TIP If you are cooking this for toddlers or children, or individuals trying to lower their salt intake, omit the salt.

Method:

1. Preheat the oven to 180 °C/160 °C fan/gas mark 4.

2. Remove the skin and bones from the hake fillets. (Place the fish on a cutting board. Use a sharp knife to cut between the flesh and skin. Start at the tail end or the corner of the fillet and carefully cut along the length of the fillet. Take care that you do not cut through the skin or cut away any flesh. Check for bones by feeling along the length of the fillet with your fingertips. If there are any bones, they can be removed using a tweezers.) Cut the hake into bite-size chunks.

3. Wash the leek, especially between the inner leaves. On a chopping board (separate to the one used for the fish), top and tail the leek and slice finely.

4. Wash the asparagus. Gently remove the woody ends, bending the end of each asparagus spear until it snaps naturally. Then cut each spear diagonally into 3 cm pieces.

5. Peel and finely chop or crush the garlic.

6. Boil the water in a kettle and pour it over the stock cube in a jug to dissolve it. Add the milk to the stock and stir. Set the liquid aside until required.

7. Preheat a large saucepan over a medium heat for 1 minute. Add the oil and butter.

8. Add the leek and sauté for about 3–4 minutes or until softened. Add the garlic and cook for 1 minute.

9. Add the rice and stir for 2–3 minutes or until it starts to look translucent.

10. Pour in enough of the stock mixture to just cover the rice. Season with the salt and pepper.

11. Allow the mixture to simmer for a few minutes. Stir occasionally, using a wooden spoon.

12. As the stock is absorbed add more of the stock mixture. Mix well to combine and continue to simmer, stirring occasionally.

13. Continue until all the stock mixture is used. This will take about 15 minutes.

14. Stir in the frozen peas and pieces of asparagus.

15. Pour the risotto into an ovenproof dish.

16. Place the hake pieces on top of the risotto.

17. Cover the dish with tinfoil and place it in the oven. Bake for 10–12 minutes or until the rice is al dente (fully cooked, but still firm).

18. While the risotto is baking, grate the Parmesan using the fine side of the grater or shave into wafer-thin slices with a vegetable peeler.

19. Remove the risotto from the oven.

20. Stir the crème fraîche into the risotto, sprinkle the Parmesan on top to garnish and serve.

HAKE, LEEK AND ASPARAGUS RISOTTO

Spicy Beef Stir-Fry with Egg Noodles

SUGGESTED AREAS OF PRACTICE

Area of Practice A: Application of Nutritional Principles | Anaemia, Pregnancy, Low-Salt Diet, Low-Fat/Low-Cholesterol Diet, Coronary Heart Disease, Teenagers, Third-Level Students

Area of Practice B: Food Preparation and Cooking Processes: Food Safety

Area of Practice D: Properties of a Food | Marinating

Serves: 4

Preparation Time: 25 minutes

Cooking Time: 15 minutes

Ingredients:

For the marinade:

- 2 cloves of garlic
- 1 red chilli
- 1 tablespoon of peanut or sesame oil
- Juice of ½ a lime
- 1 tablespoon of soy sauce
- ½ tablespoon of brown sugar
- 1 tablespoon of sweet chilli sauce

For the stir-fry:

- 3–4 minute beef steaks or 450 g of topside beef
- 1 red pepper
- 1 × 220 g packet of baby sweetcorn
- 100 g of mangetout
- 2 spring onions
- 450 g of baby spinach
- 2 tablespoons of peanut or sesame oil
- 200 g of dried medium egg noodles
- A pinch of salt and pepper

To serve:

- 1 spring onion
- 25 g of cashew nuts

TIP

If you are cooking this for individuals with coronary heart disease or those on a low-fat diet, replace the beef with chicken and replace the oil with low-calorie spray oil. Also, omit the salt and use low-salt soy sauce.

Method:

Marinade:

1. Peel the garlic clove and slice thinly.
2. Remove the stalk of the chilli. Cut the chilli lengthwise, remove the seeds and membrane, and dice finely.
3. Squeeze the juice from half a lime, using a juicer.
4. Put the garlic, chilli, oil, lime juice, soy sauce, brown sugar and sweet chilli sauce into a large bowl and combine using a fork or whisk.
5. On a separate chopping board, trim unwanted pieces from the steaks and slice into thin strips.
6. Place the meat in the marinade and mix thoroughly with a fork so that each strip is covered.
7. Cover with cling film and leave in the fridge for at least 15–20 minutes to marinate.

Vegetables:

8. While the meat is marinating, prepare the vegetables for the stir-fry. Wash the pepper, baby sweetcorn, mangetout and spring onions.
9. Cut the pepper in half lengthwise and remove the stalk, seeds and white membrane. Slice thinly into even, vertical strips.
10. Wash the spring onions, top and tail, and slice finely. Set some aside for the garnish.
11. Wash the baby spinach leaves in a colander. Empty the baby spinach onto a clean tea towel and pat dry.
12. Preheat a wok over a medium-high heat for 1 minute. Add 1 tablespoon of the oil.
13. Stir-fry the pepper strips and baby sweetcorn for 2–3 minutes.
14. Add the mangetout and diced spring onion and continue to stir-fry for 1–2 minutes.
15. Remove the vegetables from the wok and place them on a plate.

Noodles:

16. Boil a full kettle. Pour the boiling water into a large saucepan. Place the saucepan on a high heat. Carefully add the noodles to the boiling water. Stir the noodles from time to time to stop them from sticking together. Cook for 4 minutes or until al dente (fully cooked, but still firm). (You should also check the packet for instructions on cooking times.)

Final stage:

17. Remove the beef from the fridge, add another tablespoon of oil to the wok and stir-fry the beef until browned.
18. Reduce the heat to medium and add the vegetables and the washed spinach back into the wok. Toss for 1–2 minutes to heat the vegetables through and wilt the spinach.
19. Drain the noodles using a colander and rinse under cold running water.
20. Stir the drained noodles into the wok and allow them to heat. Season to taste and remove from the heat.
21. Place the stir-fry on serving plate or in bowls. Garnish with the cashew nuts and the spring onion you set aside earlier and serve.

SPICY BEEF STIR-FRY WITH EGG NOODLES

Sweet Potato, Aubergine and Chickpea Curry

SUGGESTED AREAS OF PRACTICE

Area of Practice A: Application of Nutritional Principles | Teenagers, Third-Level Students, Low-Income Family, Vegetarian, Low-Fat/Low-Cholesterol Diet, Coronary Heart Disease, High-Fibre Diet, Low-Salt Diet

Serves: 4

Preparation Time: 25 minutes

Cooking Time: 20 minutes

Ingredients:

- 1 medium aubergine
- 1 tablespoon of salt
- 1 onion
- 2 cloves of garlic
- 1 × 2½ cm piece of fresh ginger
- 1 red chilli
- 1 large sweet potato
- 1 handful of fresh coriander
- 125 g of baby spinach leaves
- 1 × 400 g can of chickpeas
- 3 tablespoons of peanut or vegetable oil
- 1 tablespoon of garam masala
- 1 × 400 ml can of coconut milk
- 1 × 400 g can of chopped tomatoes
- 300 g of brown basmati rice

To garnish:

- 1 tablespoon of Greek yoghurt
- 4 fresh coriander leaves

 TIP If you are cooking this for individuals with coronary heart disease, omit the salt and use low-fat coconut milk. If you are cooking for those trying to lower their salt intake, omit the salt.

Method:

Curry:

1. Wash the aubergine, remove the stalk and cut into 2 cm chunks. Place the aubergine in a colander and sprinkle with salt. Set aside for 10–15 minutes.
2. Top and tail the onion, remove the skin and dice finely.
3. Peel and finely chop or crush the garlic cloves.
4. Peel the ginger and grate using the fine side of the grater.
5. Remove the stalk of the chilli. Cut the chilli lengthwise, remove the seeds and membrane, and dice finely.
6. Peel the sweet potato, rinse and cut into 1 cm cubes.
7. Rinse the coriander and chop roughly.
8. Wash the baby spinach leaves in a colander. Empty the baby spinach onto a clean tea towel and pat dry.
9. Rinse the salt from the aubergine (still in the colander). Empty the aubergine onto a clean tea towel and pat dry.
10. Drain the chickpeas in a colander.
11. Preheat a large pan over a medium heat for 1 minute. Add 2 tablespoons of the oil.
12. Fry the aubergine chunks for 3–4 minutes or until golden. Lift out the aubergine with a fish slice and place it on kitchen paper on a plate to absorb excess oil.
13. Leave the pan on a medium heat and add the remaining tablespoon of oil.
14. Sauté the onion for 3–4 minutes or until soft and translucent. Add the garlic, ginger and chilli. Cook for 2 minutes.
15. Stir in the garam masala and cook for 1 minute, stirring all the time to prevent sticking.
16. Stir in the sweet potato chunks.
17. Stir in the coconut milk, tinned tomatoes and chickpeas.
18. Turn the heat up to high to bring the mixture to the boil, then reduce the heat to medium and simmer for 15–20 minutes or until the sauce has thickened.

Rice:

19. Boil a full kettle.
20. While the kettle is boiling, add the rice into a colander and rinse it under cold running water for about 1 minute to remove the starch.
21. Pour the boiling water into a large saucepan. Place the saucepan on a high heat. Carefully add the rice to the boiling water and cook for 15–20 minutes or until al dente (fully cooked, but still firm).

Final stage:

22. When the curry sauce has thickened, stir in the chopped coriander.
23. Add the spinach. Allow approximately 1–2 minutes for it to wilt and then remove the pan from the heat.
24. Drain the rice using a colander and fluff up with a fork.
25. Rinse the coriander for garnishing.
26. Place the rice in a small bowl or mould and then invert it (turn it upside down) onto a serving plate. Using a ladle, place the curry alongside the rice. Add the Greek yoghurt, garnish with a coriander leaf and serve.

SWEET POTATO, AUBERGINE AND CHICKPEA CURRY

Happy Pear Dahl

(from *The Happy Pear* by David and Stephen Flynn)

Ingredients:

- 500 g red lentils
- 2 red onions
- 3 cloves of garlic
- ½ a thumb-size piece of ginger
- 1 courgette
- 4 medium tomatoes (ideally nice and ripe)
- 3 teaspoons salt (use a decent unrefined sea salt such as Maldon)
- 2 teaspoons ground cumin
- A pinch of cayenne pepper
- 1 teaspoon ground turmeric
- 3 teaspoons medium curry powder
- 1 teaspoon freshly ground black pepper
- 3 tablespoons tamari, Bragg Liquid Aminos or soy sauce
- Juice of 1 lime
- A small bunch of fresh coriander

SUGGESTED AREAS OF PRACTICE

Area of Practice A: Application of Nutritional Principles | Teenagers, Third-Level Students, Low-Income Family, Vegetarian, Low-Fat/Low-Cholesterol Diet, Coronary Heart Disease, Low-Salt Diet

Serves: 4

Preparation Time: 15 minutes

Cooking Time: 40 minutes

TIP If you are cooking this for individuals trying to lower their salt intake or those with heart disease, omit the salt and use low-salt soy sauce.

TIP Serve with 300 g of brown basmati rice for balance.

This recipe will need to be written into your *Food Studies Practical Coursework Journal* using the detailed recipe format found in the other recipes in this book.

Method:

1. If you have time, you can soak the lentils in cold water for a few hours, but this is not essential. Drain and rinse them before using.

2. Peel and finely slice the onions, garlic and ginger.

3. Cut the courgette into bite-size pieces and roughly chop the tomatoes.

4. Sauté the onions, garlic and ginger in 4 tablespoons of water in a large pan on a high heat for 5 minutes. Stir regularly, adding more water if they start to stick to the bottom of the pan.

5. When the onions are soft, add the courgette, tomatoes and 1 teaspoon of the salt. Cover the pan and cook gently over a low heat for 5–10 minutes, stirring occasionally. If you have time, cook the vegetables for longer – the longer you cook them, the more flavourful your dahl will be.

6. Add the lentils, spices, tamari, lime juice, the remaining salt and 2 litres of water, and bring to the boil. Reduce to a low heat and simmer for 25 minutes, or until you are happy with the texture of the dahl. Stir regularly, as lentils have a tendency to stick.

7. Finely chop the coriander and sprinkle over the dahl.

8. Serve with brown rice or toasted wholemeal pitta breads, cut into soldiers. Mango chutney is also a nice accompaniment.

Pimping up your dahl!

- Add raisins and apple to sweeten it. The raisins give a nice contrasting colour.
- Baby spinach is great for colour and adds another texture.
- For a fresh accompaniment, make a simple Indian salad of finely diced red onion, tomato, cucumber and mint, with lemon juice and fresh coriander.
- For a depth of richness to your dahl, add a tin of low-fat coconut milk when putting in the lentils.

 TIP If you are using rice, you will need to explain your cooking method in your *Food Studies Practical Coursework Journal*.

HAPPY PEAR DAHL

Chicken and Mushroom Puff Pastry Pie

SUGGESTED AREAS OF PRACTICE

Area of Practice A: Application of Nutritional Principles | Toddlers/Children, Teenagers, Third-Level Students, Pregnancy, Osteoporosis, Low-Salt Diet, Older People

Area of Practice B: Food Preparation and Cooking Processes | Food Safety, Commercial Pastry: Puff

Area of Practice D: Properties of a Food | Gelatinisation

―――――――――――――

Serves: 4

Preparation Time: 20 minutes

Cooking Time: 40 minutes

Ingredients:

- 4 chicken fillets
- 1 medium leek
- 300 g of button mushrooms
- 50 g of butter
- A pinch of salt and pepper
- 50 g of flour, plus extra for dusting
- 350 ml of milk
- 100 ml of cream
- 2 sprigs of fresh tarragon
- 1 egg
- 1 × 500 g pack of puff pastry

To garnish:

- A sprig of fresh tarragon

TIP If you are cooking this for individuals trying to lower their salt intake or those with heart disease, omit the salt.

Method:

1. Preheat the oven to 200 °C/180 °C fan/gas mark 6.
2. Trim any unwanted pieces from the chicken fillets and cut into bite-size chunks.
3. Wash the leek, especially between the inner leaves. On a separate chopping board, trim off the top and bottom of the leek and slice finely.
4. Wash the mushrooms and cut into quarters.
5. Preheat a large frying pan over a medium heat for 1 minute. Add the butter.
6. When the butter has melted, season the chicken with salt and pepper and fry for 6–7 minutes until white/golden brown on the outside.
7. Stir in the sliced leek and cook for 1 minute.
8. Stir in the quartered mushrooms and cook for 3 minutes.

Roux sauce:

9. Sprinkle the flour over the ingredients in the frying pan, stir with a wooden spoon and cook for 1 minute.
10. Pour in the milk and cream and mix thoroughly. Allow the mixture to cook for 3–4 minutes or until the sauce has thickened, stirring all the time.
11. When the sauce is thickened, remove the pan from the heat. Rinse the tarragon and chop finely. Stir the chopped tarragon into the sauce.

Assembly:

12. Pour the contents of the frying pan into a 25 cm × 25 cm ovenproof dish.
13. Beat the egg in a bowl and brush onto the edges of the dish, using a pastry brush.

 TIP If you do not have a 25 cm × 25 cm dish, something similar will do. Just make sure it is ovenproof.

14. Sprinkle a little flour onto the work surface. Place the puff pastry on the work surface and sprinkle the top with a little flour. Place the rolling pin in the centre of the pastry and lightly roll the pastry. Every few rolls, sprinkle the surface of the pastry with a little more flour and rotate it to stop it from sticking to the work surface. Keep rolling until the pastry is a little bigger than the diameter of the dish. (If the pastry is pre-rolled, simply unroll from the packaging.) Lift the pastry gently and place it on top of the dish.
15. Press the puff pastry down onto the edges of the dish. Trim any excess pastry on the sides using a sharp knife. Crimp with a fork (press the fork all the way around the edge of the dish) or crimp with your fingers (use your fingers to press the pastry towards the edge of the dish). You can use the trimmings to create decorative leaves or shapes for the top of the pie.
16. Create a slit in the pastry on the top of the pie to allow the steam out during cooking.
17. Brush the pastry with the remaining beaten egg, to glaze.
18. Bake in the oven for 20 minutes or until the pastry is crisp and golden brown. Remove the pie from the oven and allow it to cool slightly.
19. Cut a slice of pie, and place it on a serving plate. Rinse the tarragon sprig, then use it to garnish the pie, and serve.

CHICKEN AND MUSHROOM PUFF PASTRY PIE

Mediterranean Quiche

SUGGESTED AREAS OF PRACTICE

Area of Practice A: Application of Nutritional Principles │ Teenagers, Active Young Person, Osteoporosis

Area of Practice B: Food Preparation and Cooking Processes │ Food Processor

Area of Practice D: Properties of a Food │ Properties of Eggs: Coagulation, Properties of Fats and Oils

Serves: 4   **Preparation Time:** 30 minutes
Cooking Time: 40 minutes

Ingredients:

Pastry:
- 200 g of plain flour, plus extra for dusting
- A pinch of salt
- 125 g of butter, plus 2 teaspoons for greasing
- 40–60 ml of cold water

Filling:
- 1 red pepper
- 1 yellow pepper
- 1 red onion
- 1 tablespoon of olive oil
- A pinch of salt and pepper
- 25 g of Parmesan cheese
- 100 ml of double cream
- 200 ml of whole milk
- 4 eggs
- 5 sun-dried tomatoes
- 100 g of chorizo

To garnish:
- A sprig of fresh parsley

Method:

Pastry:

1. Preheat the oven to 200 °C/180 °C fan/gas mark 6.
2. Insert the knife blade attachment into the bowl of the food processor and add the flour and a pinch of salt.
3. Cut the butter into 4 cm cubes and add to the flour. Lock the lid of the food processor into place.
4. Using the pulse button, process the contents until they resemble breadcrumbs.
5. Switch the food processor to a low speed and slowly add the water through the feed tube. Add just enough for the pastry to come together and form a ball, then switch off the machine. Do not over-mix or add too much liquid.
6. Remove the pastry from the processor, wrap it in cling film and rest it in the fridge while preparing the filling.
7. Wash the food processor bowl and knife blade attachment.

Filling:

8. While the pastry is resting, prepare the filling for the quiche. Cut the red and yellow peppers in half lengthwise. Remove the stalks, seeds and membranes from the peppers.
9. Insert the julienne blade into the bowl of the food processor and lock the lid into place.
10. Switch on the food processor and add the pepper halves into the feed tube, using the pusher to push the pepper onto the blade.

11. When complete, remove the pepper slices and drain on kitchen paper on a plate to absorb excess moisture.

12. Top and tail the red onion, remove the skin and cut in half. With the julienne blade still in place, switch on the food processor and add the onion halves into the feed tube, using the pusher to push them onto the blade. Remove the sliced onion from the bowl.

13. Put the sliced peppers and onion into a large bowl. Add the olive oil and season with a pinch of salt. Spread evenly on a baking tray or roasting tin and roast in the oven for 15 minutes.

Baking blind:

14. While the vegetables are roasting, grease the sides and base of a 23 cm loose-bottomed tart tin with the 2 teaspoons of butter.

15. Remove the pastry dough from the fridge. Sprinkle the work surface with flour. Place the pastry on the work surface and sprinkle the top with a little flour. Place the rolling pin in the centre of the pastry and lightly roll the pastry. Every few rolls, sprinkle the surface of the pastry with a little more flour and rotate it to stop it from sticking to the work surface. Keep rolling until the pastry is approximately 5 cm bigger than the diameter of the tart tin.

16. With your tart tin nearby, gently roll the pastry onto the rolling pin, lift, and unroll the pastry into the tart tin. Gently push the pastry into the base and sides. There will be some excess pastry hanging over the edge – do not trim it off at this stage. Use a fork to lightly prick the base of the pastry.

17. Take some baking parchment or tinfoil and gently lay it on top of the pastry. Weight it down with baking beans (or dried beans or rice).

18. Bake the pastry case blind in the oven for 15 minutes.

Assembly:

19. While the pastry is baking blind, insert the grating disc attachment into the bowl of the food processor. Switch on the food processor and add the Parmesan through the feed tube, using the pusher to push the Parmesan onto the grater. Remove the grated Parmesan and grating disc. Place the Parmesan in a bowl and set aside.

20. Remove the pastry case from the oven and remove the baking parchment or tinfoil and baking beans. Using a sharp knife, trim the excess pastry from the edges. Place the pastry case back in the oven and bake for a further 5 minutes.

21. Next, insert the knife blade attachment into the bowl of the food processor and add the cream, milk and eggs. Lock the lid into place and, using the pulse button, process the contents until smooth.

22. When the pastry case is cooked, remove it from the oven. Place the tin on a wire rack and allow the pastry to cool in the tin until required.

23. Using a sharp knife, slice each sun-dried tomato into 3–4 pieces.

24. Using a sharp knife, slice the chorizo thinly.

25. Preheat a frying pan over a medium heat for 1 minute. Add the oil.

26. Fry the chorizo for 3–4 minutes, lift out and drain on kitchen paper on a plate to absorb excess oil.

27. Scatter the peppers, onions, sun-dried tomatoes and chorizo over the pastry base.

28. Pour the mixture of cream, milk and eggs on top of the peppers, onions and chorizo.

29. Sprinkle the grated Parmesan on top.

30. Place the quiche in the oven and bake for 25 minutes or until the filling is set and the top golden.

31. When cooked, remove the quiche from the oven. Place the tin on a wire rack and allow the quiche to cool in the tin for 10 minutes before removing from the dish or slicing.

32. Remove the quiche from the tin.

33. Cut a slice of quiche and place it on a serving plate. Rinse the parsley sprig, use it to garnish the quiche, and serve.

MEDITERRANEAN QUICHE

Spinach and Feta Filo Pastry Pie

SUGGESTED AREAS OF PRACTICE

Area of Practice A: Application of Nutritional Principles | Teenagers, Active Young Person, Third-Level Students

Area of Practice B: Food Preparation and Cooking Processes | Commercial Pastry: Filo

Area of Practice D: Properties of a Food | Properties of Eggs: Coagulation

Serves: 4

Preparation Time: 20 minutes

Cooking Time: 25–30 minutes

Ingredients:

- 4 spring onions
- 1 clove of garlic
- 450 g of baby spinach
- 50 g of pine nuts
- 1 tablespoon of olive oil
- A pinch of salt and pepper
- 200 g of feta cheese
- 3 medium eggs
- 200 g of cream cheese
- 50 g of butter
- 6 sheets of filo pastry

To garnish:

- A sprig of fresh parsley

Method:

Filling:

1. Preheat the oven to 200 °C/180 °C fan/gas mark 6.
2. Wash the spring onions, top and tail, and slice finely.
3. Peel and finely chop or crush the garlic.
4. Wash the baby spinach leaves in a colander. Empty the baby spinach onto a clean tea towel and pat dry.
5. Preheat a large frying pan over a medium heat for 1 minute. Add the pine nuts and lightly toast them by moving them around the hot pan for 2–3 minutes. Once browned, remove them from the pan and set them aside until later.
6. Add the olive oil to the hot pan.
7. Add the spring onions, garlic and spinach, and season with a pinch of salt and pepper. Sauté for 3–4 minutes, tossing to ensure all the spinach is wilted.
8. Remove the spinach mixture from the frying pan and place in a colander to drain and cool.
9. Crumble the feta cheese into bite-sized pieces in a small bowl.
10. Once the spinach mixture is cooled, squeeze as much liquid as possible out of it by pressing the back of a wooden spoon against the mixture in the colander.
11. In a separate bowl or cup, beat the eggs with a whisk or fork.
12. Place the spinach mixture in a large mixing bowl and add the feta, eggs, cream cheese and pine nuts. Mix gently to combine.

Assembly:

13. Melt the butter in a small pan on a medium heat for 1–2 minutes or microwave on medium power for 30 seconds. Using a pastry brush, brush some of the butter onto the inside of a 23 cm springform tin. Place the springform tin on a baking tray until required.
14. Gently open out the filo pastry sheets. Remove one and brush the sheet with some of the melted butter.
15. Lay the sheet buttered side up in the greased dish, pressing it in against the bottom and sides. Leave the excess hanging out over the top.

> **TIP** Filo pastry is very thin and delicate. It can tear easily, so handle with care.

16. Repeat with three more sheets of pastry, brushing each with butter and overlapping them so that the inside of the tin is completely covered.
17. Place the spinach mixture on top of the pastry layers and spread it out evenly.
18. Fold the excess filo pastry over to enclose the filling.
19. Gently scrunch the remaining pastry and arrange it on top of the pie, to produce a crunchy, ruffled effect.
20. Brush the top of the pastry with the remaining melted butter.
21. Bake in the oven for 20–25 minutes until golden and crispy on top.
22. Remove the pie from the oven and carefully release it from the springform tin. Slide the pie onto a serving plate or board.
23. Cut a slice of the pie and place it on a serving plate. Rinse the sprig of parsley, use it to garnish the pie and serve.

SPINACH AND FETA FILO PASTRY PIE

Thai Salmon Fishcakes with Quinoa Salad and Sweet Potato Wedges

SUGGESTED AREAS OF PRACTICE

Area of Practice A: Application of Nutritional Principles | Active Young Person, Teenagers, Low-Salt Diet, Pregnancy, Low-Fat/Low-Cholesterol Diet, Coronary Heart Disease

Serves: 4

Preparation Time: 30 minutes

Cooking Time: 20–25 minutes

TIP

If cooking for individuals trying to lower their salt intake, omit the fish sauce, curry paste and salt. For those on a low-fat diet, replace the oils with low-calorie spray oil and serve with low-fat natural yoghurt. For those with coronary heart disease, follow all these guidelines.

Ingredients:

For the fishcakes:
- 2 salmon fillets
- 1 × 2½ cm piece of fresh ginger
- 1 clove of garlic
- 2 spring onions
- ½ a lime
- 1 handful of fresh coriander
- 1 teaspoon of Thai red curry paste
- 1 teaspoon of fish sauce
- 1 teaspoon of brown sugar
- A pinch of salt
- 1 tablespoon of peanut or sesame oil

For the quinoa salad:
- 50 g of quinoa
- 3 spring onions
- ½ a cucumber
- 1 small avocado
- ½ a lemon
- 1 × 220 g can of chickpeas
- 1 teaspoon of ground cumin
- 8–10 fresh mint leaves

For the sweet potato wedges:
- 2 large sweet potatoes
- 1 tablespoon of olive oil
- 1 teaspoon of ground cumin
- A pinch of salt

To serve:
- 1 tablespoon of natural yoghurt
- 4 fresh coriander leaves

Method:

Fishcakes:

1. Preheat the oven to 200 °C/180 °C fan/gas mark 6.
2. Insert the knife blade attachment into the bowl of a food processor.
3. Remove any skin from the salmon fillets. (Place the fish on a cutting board. Use a sharp knife to cut between the flesh and skin. Start at the tail end or the corner of the fillet and carefully cut along the length of the fillet. Take care that you do not cut through the skin or cut away any flesh. Check for bones by feeling along the length of the fillet with your fingertips. If there are any bones, they can be removed using a tweezers.)
4. Cut the salmon into large chunks.
5. On a separate chopping board, peel the ginger and grate it using the fine side of the grater.
6. Peel the garlic clove.
7. Wash the spring onions, top and tail, and slice roughly.
8. Squeeze the juice from the lime using a juicer. Measure out 1 tablespoon and set aside.
9. Rinse the coriander and chop roughly.
10. Put the salmon, grated ginger, garlic, diced spring onions, lime juice, coriander, Thai red curry paste, fish sauce, brown sugar and a pinch of salt into the bowl of the food processor. Lock the lid of the food processor into place.
11. Using the pulse button, process the contents for a few seconds, until they form a coarse paste.
12. Remove the mixture using a spatula and place in a large mixing bowl. Using wet hands, divide the mixture into 4 fishcakes (or more, depending on desired size). Put them on a plate, cover them with cling film and place them in the fridge to firm up.

Quinoa salad:

13. Boil 150 ml of water in a kettle.
14. Place the quinoa in a sieve and rinse under cold running water for 1 minute to remove its bitter coating. Place the quinoa in a medium saucepan.
15. Pour the boiling water over the quinoa and cook on a medium heat for 15–20 minutes or until the germ has slightly separated from the seed and it is al dente (fully cooked, but still firm).
16. While the quinoa is cooking, wash the spring onions, top and tail, and slice finely. Place the spring onions in a large bowl.
17. Wash the cucumber, cut lengthwise, dice finely and add to the bowl.
18. Cut the avocado in half and remove the stone. Scoop out the flesh of the avocado with a large spoon. Cut into 1 cm cubes and place in the bowl.
19. Squeeze the juice from half a lemon using a juicer and add to the bowl.
20. Once the quinoa is cooked, drain using a sieve and rinse under cold running water to cool. Set the quinoa aside to cool further.
21. Drain the chickpeas in a colander and add them to the bowl, along with the teaspoon of ground cumin.
22. Wash the mint leaves, chop finely and add to the bowl.
23. Mix the spring onions, cucumber, avocado, lemon juice, chickpeas (with cumin) and mint leaves together.
24. Add the cooled quinoa and mix thoroughly. Cover the bowl with cling film and place in the fridge until ready to serve. ➢

THAI SALMON FISHCAKES WITH QUINOA SALAD AND SWEET POTATO WEDGES

Wedges:

25. Scrub the skin of the sweet potatoes in water and rinse them.

26. Cut each sweet potato into wedges and place in a large bowl. Add the olive oil and cumin and mix with a wooden spoon to coat well. Season with a pinch of salt.

27. Place the wedges on a baking tray, skin-side down, ensuring there is space between each wedge. Bake in the oven for 15–20 minutes or until lightly browned and softened.

Final stage:

28. While the sweet potato wedges are cooking, remove the fishcakes from the fridge.

29. Preheat a large frying pan over a medium heat for 1 minute. Add the oil.

30. Gently place the fishcakes onto the frying pan, using a fish slice to lift them from the plate to the pan.

31. Fry for 3–4 minutes, until browned on one side. Turn the fishcake and repeat on the other side. Lift the fishcake out with a fish slice and drain on kitchen paper on a plate to remove excess oil.

32. Remove the sweet potato wedges from the oven and drain on kitchen paper on a plate to remove excess oil.

33. Place the fishcakes on a serving plate and serve with a portion of quinoa salad and some sweet potato wedges. Rinse the coriander leaves. Place a spoon of natural yoghurt on the side of the plate and garnish with the coriander leaves.

Chive and Apple Sliders with Spicy Ketchup and Homemade Chips

SUGGESTED AREAS OF PRACTICE

Area of Practice A: Application of Nutritional Principles | Toddlers/Children, Teenagers, Third-Level Students, Anaemia, Pregnancy, Low-Salt Diet, Low-Income Family

Area of Practice B: Food Preparation and Cooking Processes: Food Safety

Serves: 4
Preparation Time: 25 minutes
Cooking Time: 20–25 minutes

Ingredients:

For the sliders:
- 500 g of lean minced beef
- ½ a red onion
- 1 tablespoon of fresh chives
- 1 teaspoon of Worcestershire sauce
- 1 eating apple (e.g. Braeburn, Pink Lady, etc.)

For the ketchup:
- 125 ml of tomato ketchup
- ½ a red onion
- 60 ml of white wine vinegar
- A pinch of dried chilli flakes
- 2 teaspoons of brown sugar

For the chips:
- 4 large Rooster potatoes
- 2 tablespoons of olive oil
- A pinch of salt

To serve:
- Mini burger buns or small soft bread rolls
- Your choice of toppings: tomato, sliced cheese, red onion rings, lettuce, etc.

TIP If you are cooking this for toddlers or children, omit the chilli flakes and salt. If cooking for individuals trying to lower their salt intake, omit the salt and Worcestershire sauce.

Method:

Sliders:

1. Preheat the oven to 200 °C/180 °C fan/gas mark 6.
2. Place the minced beef in a large mixing bowl.
3. Top and tail the onion, remove the skin and dice finely. Add half of the onion to the minced beef and keep the other half for the ketchup.
4. Rinse the chives, chop finely and add to the onion and minced beef.
5. Add the Worcestershire sauce.
6. Peel the apples and grate them using the fine side of the grater. Add the grated apples to the bowl.
7. Mix the contents of the bowl using a fork.
8. Using wet hands, shape the contents of the bowl into approximately 8 small sliders (mini burgers).
9. Place the sliders on a plate, cover them with cling film and leave them in the fridge to firm up.

Ketchup:

10. While the sliders are chilling, make the spicy ketchup. Put the ketchup, onion, vinegar, chilli flakes and brown sugar into a small saucepan.
11. Stir to mix, then cook on a medium heat for 15–20 minutes or until the sauce has thickened.
12. Remove the saucepan from the heat and allow the ketchup to cool.

Chips:

13. Peel the potatoes and rinse under cold running water.
14. Cut each potato in half lengthwise and then cut into long, thin chip shapes.
15. Place the chopped potatoes in a large bowl, add the olive oil and mix well with a wooden spoon. Season with a pinch of salt.
16. Place the chopped potatoes on a baking tray, ensuring there is space between each chip, and bake in the oven for 20 minutes or until lightly browned and softened.

Final stage:

17. While the chips are cooking, remove the sliders from the fridge.
18. Preheat the grill to a medium-high heat.
19. Place the sliders onto a grill pan and grill for 4–5 minutes on one side. Turn the sliders and grill for 4–5 minutes on the other side. Lift the sliders off the grill pan with a fish slice and drain on kitchen paper on a plate to remove excess oil.
20. Turn the grill pan down to a low heat and toast the mini burger buns for 1–2 minutes or until light brown.
21. Remove the chips from the oven and drain on kitchen paper to remove excess oil.
22. Place a slider on the base of a bun. Add some spicy ketchup and your choice of toppings. Top with the other half of the bun. Serve with a portion of the homemade chips and a dollop of ketchup.

Note: If using this recipe, you must describe how you prepared and added the chosen burger toppings in the Implementation section of your Food Studies Journal.

Lemon Meringue Pie

SUGGESTED AREAS OF PRACTICE

Area of Practice C: Food Technology | Home Baking

Area of Practice D: Properties of a Food | Properties of Starch: Gelatinisation, Properties of Eggs: Aeration, Properties of Protein: Denaturation, Properties of Fats and Oils

Serves: 6–8

Preparation Time: 55 minutes

Cooking Time: 18–20 minutes

 TIP You will need a total of 5 eggs for this recipe.

Ingredients:

For the pastry:
- 110 g of butter, plus 2 teaspoons for greasing
- 175 g of plain flour, plus extra for dusting
- 40 g of icing sugar
- 1 egg yolk
- 1–2 tablespoons of cold water

For the lemon curd:
- 2 lemons
- 90 g of caster sugar
- 2 tablespoons of cornflour
- 80 ml of water
- 85 g of butter
- 3 egg yolks
- 1 whole egg

For the meringue:
- 4 egg whites, at room temperature
- 200 g of caster sugar
- 2 tablespoons of cornflour

Method:

Pastry:

1. Preheat the oven to 200 °C/180 °C fan/gas mark 6.
2. Grease a 23 cm loose-bottomed, fluted tart tin with the 2 teaspoons of butter.
3. Sieve the flour and icing sugar into a large mixing bowl.
4. Cut the butter into cubes. Using your fingertips, rub it into the flour and icing sugar until it resembles coarse breadcrumbs.
5. Separate an egg, setting aside the egg white for the meringue.
6. Add the egg yolk and a tablespoon of the water to the mixture. Using a cold knife, mix to bring the pastry together until it forms a large dough ball in the centre of the bowl. You may need to add a little more water for it to bind together.
7. Remove the pastry from the bowl, wrap it in cling film and place it in the fridge to rest.

> **TIP**
> This pastry can be made in a food processor. Insert the knife blade attachment into the bowl of the food processor. Place the flour, icing sugar and butter in the bowl. Use the pulse button to process the ingredients until they resemble breadcrumbs. Slowly add the egg yolk and water through the feed tube until the pastry comes together.

Lemon curd:

8. Wash the lemons. Remove the zest using the fine side of the grater.
9. Squeeze the juice from the lemons using a juicer and measure 120 ml in a measuring jug.
10. Place the lemon zest, sugar and cornflour into a large saucepan.
11. Gradually add in the lemon juice and water. Stir until combined.
12. Place the saucepan on a medium heat and cook the mixture for 3–4 minutes, stirring all the time, until the mixture thickens.
13. Remove the saucepan from the heat and add in the butter, mixing until it is melted and fully combined.
14. Separate 3 eggs and place the egg yolks in a small bowl. Add the egg whites to the one you set aside earlier for the meringue.
15. Add the remaining whole egg to the egg yolks and beat together using a fork. Add this to the lemon curd in the saucepan. Use a wooden spoon to mix until smooth.
16. Return the saucepan to a medium heat and cook (stirring all the time) for another 2–3 minutes, or until the mixture has thickened and is bubbling gently.
17. Remove the saucepan from the heat and set aside to cool.

Baking Blind:

18. Remove the pastry dough from the fridge.

19. Sprinkle the work surface with flour. Place the pastry on the work surface and sprinkle the top with a little flour. Place the rolling pin in the centre of the pastry and lightly roll the pastry. Every few rolls, sprinkle the surface of the pastry with a little more flour and rotate it to stop it from sticking to the work surface. Keep rolling until the pastry is approximately 5 cm bigger than the diameter of the tart tin.

20. With your tart tin nearby, gently roll the pastry onto the rolling pin, lift, and unroll the pastry into the tart tin. Gently push it into the base and sides. There will be some excess pastry hanging over the edge – do not trim it off at this stage. Use a fork to lightly prick the base of the pastry several times.

21. Take some baking parchment or tinfoil and gently lay it on top. Weight the parchment or foil down with ceramic baking beans (or dried beans or rice).

22. Bake the pastry case blind in the oven for 15 minutes.

Meringue:

23. While the pastry is baking blind, make the meringue.

24. In a large bowl, using a hand-held electric whisk, whisk the 4 egg whites you set aside earlier on high speed until they form soft peaks. ('Soft peaks' means that, when you lift up the beaters, the 'peaks' of the egg white should flop over and be just starting to hold.)

25. Add half the sugar, one spoonful at a time, whisking all the time.

26. Add the rest of the sugar, spoonful by spoonful, continuing to whisk until the meringue is very thick and forms stiff peaks. ('Stiff peaks' means that, when you turn the whisk upside down, the 'peaks' of egg white should stand up straight and, when you tilt the bowl, the contents should not move.)

27. Sieve in the cornflour and fold in using a spatula. ('Folding' means to stir in very gently, making sure you retain the air you whipped into the egg whites.)

Final stage:

28. Remove the pastry case from the oven and remove the baking parchment and baking beans. Using a sharp knife, trim the excess pastry. Place the tin back in the oven and bake for a further 5 minutes.

29. Remove the pastry case from the oven. Place the tin on a wire rack and allow the pastry to cool in the tin for 5 minutes.

30. Pour the lemon curd into the partially cooled pastry case.

31. Gently place large spoonfuls of the meringue on top of the lemon curd, until the curd is fully covered. Gently spread it out until it just touches the pastry case.

32. Use a spoon to swirl the meringue and form peaks.

33. Bake in the oven for 18–20 minutes or until the meringue is crisp and slightly golden.

34. Remove the pie from the oven. Place the tin on a wire rack and allow the pie to cool completely in the tin.

35. When the pie is completely cool, remove it from the tin.

36. To serve, cut a slice from the pie and place on a serving plate.

LEMON MERINGUE PIE

White Chocolate, Strawberry and Oreo Cheesecake

SUGGESTED AREAS OF PRACTICE

Area of Practice B: Food Preparation and Cooking Processes | Gelatine
_____

Serves: 10

Preparation Time: 25–30 minutes

Cooking Time: 5–12 hours to chill

Ingredients:

For the base:
- 100 g of butter
- 300 g of Oreo cookies

For the filling:
- 100 g of Oreo cookies
- 10 fresh strawberries
- 350 g of full-fat cream cheese, at room temperature
- 100 g of caster sugar
- 1 teaspoon of vanilla extract
- 150 g of white chocolate
- 3 tablespoons of water
- 1 × 11 g sachet of powdered gelatine
- 160 ml of whipping cream

To decorate:
- 60g of Oreo cookies
- 10 fresh strawberries

TIP 3 × 154 g packets of Oreo cookies are sufficient for this recipe.

Method:

Base:

1. Melt the butter in a medium saucepan on a medium heat, or microwave on high power for 30 seconds.
2. Insert the knife blade attachment into the bowl of a food processor.
3. Place the Oreos in the food processor. Lock the lid into place. Using the pulse button, process the contents until they resemble fine breadcrumbs. Transfer into a large mixing bowl.
4. Add the melted butter to the Oreos and mix with a wooden spoon until fully combined.
5. Add the Oreo mixture to a 23 cm springform tin and press it down firmly, using the bottom of a glass or ramekin.
6. Place the biscuit base in the fridge to chill while you make the filling.

 TIP Turn the base of the springform tin upside down. This creates a smooth base, which makes the cheesecake easier to cut and remove from the tin.

Filling:

7. Chop the Oreos into chunks and set aside.
8. Boil the kettle.
9. Rinse and hull the strawberries. (Use a small, sharp knife to cut around the stalk and remove the hard, white flesh called the 'hull'.) Cut 10 strawberries into quarters for the filling. Slice the other 10 strawberries in half and set aside for decorating the top.
10. Using a wooden spoon, beat the cream cheese, sugar and vanilla extract together in a large bowl until smooth.
11. Pour a little hot water from the kettle into a saucepan and place on a medium heat. Set a bowl over the saucepan. Make sure that the water does not touch the bottom of the bowl. Break the white chocolate into squares and place in the bowl. Leave on a medium heat for 3–4 minutes or until the chocolate has melted.
12. Turn off the heat, remove the bowl from the saucepan and allow the melted chocolate to cool for 4–5 minutes. Gently stir the chocolate into the cream cheese mixture using a wooden spoon.
13. Reboil the kettle. Put 3 tablespoons of the hot water into a small bowl or jug, and sprinkle in the gelatine. Stir well until the gelatine has dissolved. If it does not dissolve, stand the bowl into a saucepan of hot water and heat on a medium heat for 3–4 minutes until no grains of gelatine remain.
14. Pour the gelatine into the cream cheese and chocolate mixture and mix to fully combine.
15. In a separate large mixing bowl, using a hand-held electric whisk, whip the cream until it starts to hold its shape.
16. Add a spoonful of the cream to the cream cheese and chocolate mixture and use a spoon or whisk to stir vigorously until combined. This lightens the mixture and makes it easier to fold in the rest of the cream.
17. Gently fold in the cream, then the chopped Oreos and quartered strawberries.

Assembly:

18. Remove the cheesecake base from the fridge. Pour the cheesecake filling onto the base, smoothing out the top with a spoon or spatula.
19. Cut the remaining Oreos into quarters. Arrange the quarters on top of the cheesecake with the rounded side facing up, leaving a gap between each. Sprinkle any remaining biscuit crumbs over the top.
20. Place the halved strawberries in between each piece of Oreo.
21. Refrigerate for at least 5 hours or until set. It is best left overnight.
22. To serve, cut a slice from the cheesecake and place on a serving plate.

WHITE CHOCOLATE, STRAWBERRY AND OREO CHEESECAKE

Lemon Panna Cotta with Raspberry Coulis and Shortbread Biscuits

SUGGESTED AREAS OF PRACTICE

Area of Practice B: Food Preparation and Cooking Processes | Gelatine

Area of Practice C: Food Technology | Home Baking

Serves: 4 **Preparation Time:** 40 minutes

Cooking Time: 15 minutes, plus 5–12 hours to set

Ingredients:

For the panna cotta:
- 1 lemon
- 2 leaves of gelatine
- 400 ml of double cream
- 100 ml of milk
- 130 g of caster sugar

For the shortbread biscuits:
- 110 g of plain white flour, plus extra for dusting
- 1 × 2 cm piece of vanilla pod
- 75 g of butter
- 40 g of caster sugar, plus 2 teaspoons to sprinkle on top

For the raspberry coulis:
- 125 g of raspberries
- ½ tablespoon of icing sugar

Method:

Panna cotta:

1. Place the pudding moulds or small glasses on a flat baking tray.
2. Wash the lemon. Remove the zest using the fine side of the grater.
3. Squeeze the juice from the lemon using a juicer.
4. Soak the gelatine leaves in a bowl of cold water and set aside for at least 4 minutes.
5. Put the cream, milk and sugar into a large saucepan on a medium heat and bring the mixture to the boil.

6. When the cream mixture comes to the boil, add the lemon juice and zest, and mix well with a wooden spoon. Reduce the heat to medium and simmer for 2–3 minutes or until the mixture has reduced slightly, then remove the saucepan from the heat.

7. Take the softened gelatine leaves out of the water and squeeze out any excess water.

8. Stir the gelatine leaves into the hot cream until they have dissolved. Set aside until the mixture has cooled slightly.

9. When the mixture has cooled slightly, strain the mixture through a sieve into a jug.

10. Carefully pour the mixture into the glasses. Place them in the fridge for at least 5 hours, or overnight.

Shortbread biscuits:

11. While the panna cotta is setting, make the shortbread biscuits and raspberry coulis.

12. Preheat the oven to 180 °C/160 °C fan/gas mark 4.

13. Line a baking tray with a sheet of baking parchment or silicone paper.

14. Sieve the flour into a large mixing bowl.

15. Place the vanilla pod on a chopping board and use a sharp knife to split it open. Scrape out the seeds with the back of the knife, add them to the flour and mix through.

16. Cut the butter into small cubes. Add the cubes of butter and the sugar to the flour.

17. Rub the butter and sugar into the flour, using your fingertips, until it resembles coarse breadcrumbs.

18. Press the mixture into a large ball. Do not add any liquid.

19. Sprinkle the work surface with flour and tip the dough out. Use your hands to bring the dough together, kneading only enough to form a cohesive ball. Handle the dough as little as possible to give the finished biscuits a light, crumbly texture.

20. Sprinkle the top of the dough with a little flour. Place a rolling pin in the centre of the dough and lightly roll the dough. Every few rolls, sprinkle the surface of the dough with a little more flour and rotate it to stop it from sticking to the work surface. Keep rolling until the dough is 3 mm thick.

21. Use cookie cutters or a knife to cut out biscuit shapes. Continue until all of the dough has been used. You will need to tidy the scraps, re-roll and cut out more biscuits.

22. Carefully place the biscuits on the baking tray, leaving a space of about 1 cm between each biscuit.

23. Sprinkle each biscuit with a little caster sugar.

24. Bake in the oven for 15 minutes or until lightly golden.

Raspberry coulis:

25. Rinse the raspberries in a colander and remove any bruised or damaged fruit. Place them in a medium saucepan.

26. Sieve the icing sugar into the saucepan.

27. Cook the raspberries and sugar on a medium heat for 3–4 minutes or until they start to break down.

28. Insert the knife blade attachment into the bowl of the food processor. Add the contents of the saucepan into the bowl.

29. Lock the lid into place. Using the pulse button, process the contents until smooth.

30. Pass the purée through a sieve, into a bowl, to remove the raspberry seeds. Set the coulis aside until cool.

Assembly:

31. Remove the shortbread from the oven and place the baking tray on a wire rack. Allow the biscuits to cool on the baking tray for 5 minutes. Then, carefully remove the biscuits from the tray and place them on the wire rack to cool completely.

32. Remove the panna cotta from the fridge.

33. Spoon the raspberry coulis into the top of each glass. If you are using pudding moulds, dip them into a bowl of hot water for 10 seconds (ensuring no water touches the contents) and invert them (turn them upside down) onto a plate to unmould. Spoon the raspberry coulis over the panna cotta.

34. Serve with two shortbread biscuits.

Molten Chocolate Microwave Cake

SUGGESTED AREAS OF PRACTICE

Area of Practice B: Food Preparation and Cooking Processes | Microwave

Serves: 6

Preparation Time: 15 minutes

Cooking Time: 6 minutes, plus 5 minutes' standing time

Ingredients:

For the chocolate sauce:
- 110 g of soft light brown sugar
- 150 ml of cold water
- 2 tablespoons of cocoa

For the cake:
- 110 g of self-raising flour
- 2 tablespoons of cocoa
- A pinch of salt
- 110 g of caster sugar
- 55 g of butter, plus 2 teaspoons for greasing
- 1 egg
- 100 ml of milk
- 1 teaspoon of vanilla extract

To serve:
- 1 scoop of vanilla ice cream per person

Method:

Chocolate sauce:

1. Place the brown sugar and water in a microwave-safe bowl. Place the bowl in the microwave for 1 minute on high power, to melt the sugar.
2. Remove the bowl from the microwave and stir with a whisk until the sugar is completely dissolved.
3. Sieve in the cocoa. Stir until smooth and set aside until needed.

Chocolate cake:

4. Sieve the flour and cocoa into a large mixing bowl.
5. Add the salt and caster sugar and stir well to combine.
6. Put the butter into a microwave-safe bowl and place in the microwave on high power for 30 seconds to melt.
7. In a measuring jug, beat the egg with a whisk or fork. Add the milk, vanilla extract and melted butter. Mix well.
8. Pour the egg mix into the dry ingredients and mix well until everything is combined.

Assembly:

9. Grease a microwave-safe container (e.g. a 23 cm Pyrex dish) with the 2 teaspoons of butter. Pour half the cake batter into the dish.
10. Pour half the chocolate sauce over the cake batter and prod the batter with a fork to allow the sauce to seep through.
11. Add the remaining batter, followed by the remaining sauce. Again, prod the batter with a fork to allow the sauce to seep through.
12. Place in the microwave and heat on high power (700–800 W) for 6 minutes, until the batter has set and the cake appears sponge-like on top.
13. Once cooked, remove the cake from the microwave and allow it to stand for 5 minutes, during which time the cake will continue to cook.
14. Place a portion of the cake on a serving plate. Serve with a scoop of vanilla ice cream.

 TIP This may also be served with the hot chocolate sauce from page 123.

MOLTEN CHOCOLATE MICROWAVE CAKE

Raspberry Ripple Ice Cream (Custard-based)

SUGGESTED AREAS OF PRACTICE

Area of Practice C: Food Technology | Ice Cream

Serves: Yields 1 litre of ice cream

Preparation Time: 30 minutes

Cooking Time: 20 minutes to churn and 1 hour to freeze

Ingredients:

For the raspberry sauce:
- 400 g of fresh raspberries
- 80 g of caster sugar
- 45 ml of water

For the vanilla custard ice cream:
- 6 eggs
- 500 ml of double cream
- 250 ml of whole milk
- 1 vanilla pod
- 120 g of caster sugar

To garnish:
- 4 fresh mint leaves

Method:

1. If using an ice-cream maker, place the bowl of the ice-cream maker in the freezer for at least 12–15 hours beforehand.

Raspberry sauce:

2. Rinse the raspberries in a colander and remove any bruised or damaged fruit.
3. Place the raspberries, sugar and water in a saucepan.
4. Place the saucepan on a high heat and bring to the boil. When it has come to the boil, immediately reduce the heat to medium. Simmer for 6–8 minutes or until the fruit has softened and begun to break down. Stir regularly.
5. Remove the saucepan from the heat and pass the fruit through a sieve, into a bowl, to remove the raspberry seeds.
6. Return the strained raspberry liquid to the saucepan. Place on a medium heat to simmer for 5 minutes or until the mixture thickens and becomes a syrup.
7. Remove from the heat and set aside to cool completely.

Vanilla custard ice cream:

8. While the coulis is cooling, make the vanilla ice cream.
9. Separate the eggs and put the yolks into a large mixing bowl.

 TIP Do not throw away the egg whites, as they can be kept for making meringues.

10. Pour the cream and milk into a medium saucepan.
11. Cut the vanilla pod in half with a sharp knife and, using the knife, scrape out the seeds. Add these to the cream and milk mixture.
12. Place the saucepan on a medium heat until hot but not boiling. At this point, remove the saucepan from the heat and set aside.
13. Add the sugar to the egg yolks in the mixing bowl. Using a hand-held electric whisk, whisk on a high speed until pale and creamy.
14. Reduce the speed to slow. Slowly pour in the cream/milk mixture, whisking at all times.
15. Pour the custard back into the saucepan and return to a medium heat until the mixture begins to slightly bubble and steam (but not boil) and thicken. (If using a thermometer, 80 °C is the perfect temperature.) It should be thick enough to coat the back of a spoon. This should take approximately 4 minutes.
16. Remove the saucepan from the heat. Pour the custard into a jug or bowl. Cover it with cling film. Allow the custard to cool to room temperature, then place it in the fridge to cool completely.
17. Once the custard has cooled, remove it from the fridge.
18. Remove the bowl of the ice-cream maker from the freezer.
19. Pour the custard into the bowl of the ice-cream maker.
20. Churn the ice cream for 15–20 minutes in the ice-cream maker, according to the ice-cream maker's instructions.
21. Use a spatula to transfer the ice cream into a 1 litre container. Add the cooled raspberry sauce and swirl into the ice cream, using a skewer to create a ripple effect.
22. Place the rippled ice cream in the freezer to set for at least an hour.
23. When set, serve a scoop of ice cream in each bowl. Rinse the mint leaves and use to garnish the ice cream.

TIP If you do not have access to an ice-cream maker, you can still make the ice cream. Pour the mixture into a 1 litre container and put it in the freezer. After 1 hour, remove the mixture and mix with a fork or hand-held electric whisk to break up any large ice crystals. Return it to the freezer. Remove and mix once an hour for 3–4 hours, after which time it should have reached the desired consistency. Add the cooled raspberry sauce and swirl into the ice cream, using a skewer to create a ripple effect. Return to the freezer to set for at least an hour.

RASPBERRY RIPPLE ICE CREAM (CUSTARD-BASED)

Pistachio and Raspberry Meringue Cake

SUGGESTED AREAS OF PRACTICE

Area of Practice C: Food Technology | Home Baking

Area of Practice D: Properties of a Food | Aeration, Properties of Eggs, Denaturation

---

Serves: 6–8

Preparation Time: 30 minutes

Cooking Time: 50 minutes, plus at least 30 minutes' cooling time

Ingredients:

For the meringue:

- 100 g of pistachios without shells (approx. 200 g with shells)
- 4 egg whites, at room temperature
- 225 g of caster sugar
- 2 teaspoons of cornflour
- 1 teaspoon of white wine vinegar
- A pinch of salt

For the filling:

- 400 ml of double cream
- 400 g of fresh raspberries

To garnish:

- 1 tablespoon of icing sugar
- 6 fresh mint leaves

Method:

Meringue:

1. Preheat the oven to 150 °C/130 °C fan/gas mark 2.
2. Line two baking trays with baking parchment and draw a 25 cm diameter circle on each sheet. Turn the paper over to avoid getting pencil marks on the meringue discs later. You should still be able to see the circles you have drawn.
3. Remove the pistachios from their shells.
4. Insert the knife blade attachment into the bowl of the food processor. Add the pistachios. Lock the lid into place. Using the pulse button, process the pistachios until finely ground. Set aside until needed.
5. Separate the eggs and place the whites into a large, clean mixing bowl.
6. Using a hand-held electric whisk, whisk the egg whites on high speed until soft peaks form. ('Soft peaks' means that, when you lift up the beaters, the 'peaks' of the egg white should flop over and be just starting to hold.)
7. Add one-third of the caster sugar and whisk until the mixture begins to look thick and glossy. Add another third and whisk. Finally, add the remaining caster sugar and whisk until the meringue is very thick and forms stiff peaks. ('Stiff peaks' means that, when you lift up the beaters, the 'peaks' of egg white should stand up straight and, when you tilt the bowl, the contents should not move.)
8. Sieve in the cornflour. Add the vinegar and a pinch of salt and gently fold them in. ('Folding' means to stir in very gently, making sure you retain the air you whipped into the egg whites.)
9. Fold in the ground pistachios, using the same method.
10. Spoon the meringue mixture into the centre of each circle on the baking parchment and spread them out, using the spoon or a spatula, until two meringue discs are formed.
11. Place in the oven and bake for 50 minutes or until crisp and lightly coloured. Turn off the heat and allow the meringue discs to cool in the oven for at least 30 minutes.

 TIP Do not throw away the egg yolks. They can be kept in the fridge for 2–3 days and used to make rich shortcrust pastry, mayonnaise or lemon curd.

Filling:

12. Place the cream in a large mixing bowl. Using a hand-held electric whisk, whip the cream until soft peaks form.
13. Rinse the raspberries in a colander and remove any bruised or damaged fruit. Leave to drain for 1 minute.

Assembly:

14. Remove the completely cooled meringue discs from the oven and gently transfer onto two wire racks with the bottom sides facing up. Gently pull off the baking parchment.
15. Place one meringue disc on a serving plate with the flat side facing up, spread half the cream onto it and add half the raspberries. Then place the other meringue layer on top of this with the flat side facing down. Top it with the remaining cream and raspberries.
16. Dust with icing sugar. Garnish with mint leaves and serve.

PISTACHIO AND RASPBERRY MERINGUE CAKE

Profiteroles with Hot Chocolate Sauce

SUGGESTED AREAS OF PRACTICE

Area of Practice B: Food Preparation and Cooking Processes | Choux Pastry

Serves: 6

Preparation Time: 25–30 minutes

Cooking Time: 20–25 minutes

Ingredients:

For the choux pastry:
- 2 teaspoons of butter (for greasing)
- 115 g of plain flour
- A pinch of salt
- 200 ml of cold water
- 4 teaspoons of caster sugar
- 85 g of butter
- 3 medium eggs

For the filling:
- 200 ml of double cream
- ½ fresh vanilla pod

For the hot chocolate sauce:
- 200 g dark or milk chocolate
- 70 ml of cream
- 30 g of butter
- 2 tablespoons of golden syrup

Method:

Choux pastry:

1. Preheat the oven to 200 °C/180 °C fan/gas mark 6. Lightly grease a sheet of baking parchment or silicone paper. Place it on a baking tray with the greased side facing upwards.
2. Place a small roasting tin in the bottom of the oven.
3. Sieve the flour onto another sheet of baking paper. Add the salt to the flour.
4. Place the water, sugar and butter in a large saucepan. Heat gently on a low heat until the butter has melted.
5. Turn the heat up to high until the mixture comes to the boil.

6. When it has come to the boil, remove the saucepan from the heat. Quickly add the flour and salt all in one go using the baking paper as a chute.

7. Beat the mixture vigorously with a wooden spoon until a smooth paste is formed and the mixture comes away from the sides of the pan.

8. Return the saucepan to a low heat for about 30 seconds to allow the mixture to dry out. Stir it gently.

9. Remove the saucepan from the heat and leave the mixture to cool for 5–8 minutes.

10. Beat the eggs in a small bowl using a whisk or fork.

11. Once the mixture has cooled, add the beaten eggs a little at a time and beat vigorously with a wooden spoon until the mixture is smooth and has a soft dropping consistency. (You may not need to use all the beaten egg.)

12. Place the piping bag, fitted with a plain 1 cm nozzle, into a large glass. This will make it easier to add the choux pastry. Fold out the open end of the piping bag, to make a cuff. Fill the piping bag with the choux pastry.

13. Pipe the mixture into small mounds across the baking sheet, leaving a 2½ cm space between each ball for it to expand.

14. Dip a clean finger in a small bowl of water and gently rub the top of each ball.

15. Place the baking tray in the oven. Pour half a cup of water into the roasting tin at the bottom of the oven and quickly shut the door. (The steam created will help the pastry rise.)

16. Bake the profiteroles for 10 minutes, then reduce the heat to 190 °C and bake for another 10–15 minutes or until golden brown.

Filling:

17. While the profiteroles are baking, make the cream filling. Place the cream in a large mixing bowl. Using a hand-held electric whisk, whip the cream until it forms soft peaks. ('Soft peaks' means that, when you lift up the beaters, the 'peaks' should flop over and be just starting to hold.)

18. Place the vanilla pod (½) on a chopping board and use a sharp knife to split it open. Scrape out the seeds with the back of the knife and add to the cream. Stir to combine.

19. Place the piping bag, fitted with a plain nozzle, into a large glass. This will make it easier to add the cream. Fold out the open end of the piping bag, to make a cuff. Fill the piping bag with the cream. Set it aside until ready.

Hot chocolate sauce:

20. Break the chocolate into pieces.

21. Put the cream and broken chocolate into a medium saucepan. Place the saucepan on a low heat, stirring occasionally, for about 5 minutes or until the chocolate has melted.

22. Add the butter and golden syrup and stir until a thick chocolate sauce is formed. Take the saucepan off the heat. Set the sauce aside until needed.

Assembly:

23. Remove the profiteroles from the oven and turn off the oven.

24. Prick the base of each profiterole with a skewer or cocktail stick. Place the profiteroles back onto the baking sheet with the hole in the base facing upwards and return to the oven for five minutes.

25. Remove the profiteroles from the oven and place them on a wire rack to cool.

26. When completely cooled, pipe cream into each profiterole until they are completely filled.

27. Arrange the profiteroles on a serving plate in a pyramid shape. Pour over the hot chocolate sauce and serve.

PROFITEROLES WITH HOT CHOCOLATE SAUCE

Salted Caramel Chocolate Cupcakes

SUGGESTED AREAS OF PRACTICE

Area of Practice C: Food Technology | Home Baking: Muffins and Cupcakes

Area of Practice D: Properties of a Food | Properties of Sugar: Caramelisation, Properties of Eggs: Aeration

Serves: 14–16

Preparation Time: 30 minutes

Cooking Time: 20–25 minutes

Ingredients:

For the salted caramel sauce:
- 250 g of caster sugar
- 100 ml of cold water
- 120 ml of double cream
- 100 g of butter
- 1 teaspoon of sea salt

For the chocolate cupcakes:
- 170 g of plain flour
- 50 g of cocoa powder, sieved
- 1 tablespoon of baking powder
- 70 g of butter, at room temperature
- 225 g of caster sugar
- ¼ teaspoon of salt
- 210 ml of whole milk
- 2 eggs

For the buttercream icing:
- 200 g of butter, at room temperature
- 400 g of icing sugar
- ½ teaspoon of vanilla extract

Method:

Salted caramel sauce:

1. Place the caster sugar and the water in a large, heavy, wide saucepan.

2. Place the saucepan on a high heat until the sugar melts and starts to bubble. It is very important that you do not stir the caramel, as this will cause the sugar to crystallise. It is also very important that you do not taste or touch the caramel, as it is extremely hot.

3. Allow the mixture to bubble on a high heat for 5–7 minutes or until the colour begins to change and caramelisation occurs. Swirl the pan at intervals to mix. Keep a watchful eye on the caramel. Do not leave the saucepan unattended, as caramelisation can occur in seconds.

4. When the caramel is a dark amber colour, it is ready. Take the saucepan off the heat.

5. Using a wooden spoon, stir in the cream and butter slowly, until the mixture is glossy and smooth.

6. Mix in the sea salt and set aside until needed.

Chocolate cupcakes:

7. Preheat the oven to 170 °C/150 °C fan/gas mark 3.

8. Line 2 muffin tins with 14–16 paper muffin cases.

9. Put the flour, cocoa powder, baking powder, butter and caster sugar into a large mixing bowl. Using a hand-held electric whisk, mix until they resemble breadcrumbs.

10. Mix the milk and eggs together in a jug, using a whisk or fork.

11. Gradually add half the liquid to the contents of the bowl, combining with the electric whisk on a slow speed.

12. Increase the speed of the electric whisk to medium and beat until the batter is smooth.

13. Turn off the whisk and set it down. Scrape down the sides of the bowl with a spatula. Turn the whisk back on, to a low speed. Slowly pour in the remaining liquid, combining with the electric whisk until the batter is smooth.

14. Scoop the batter into the prepared muffin cases, filling each case two-thirds full. The batter will be very liquid in consistency. Using an ice-cream scoop for this is convenient and will result in even cupcakes. If an ice-cream scoop is not available, pour the mixture into a jug and pour it into the cases.

15. Bake the cupcakes in the oven for 20–25 minutes or until the sponge bounces back when lightly touched.

Salted caramel buttercream icing:

16. While the cupcakes are baking, make the buttercream icing.

17. Place the butter in a large mixing bowl and beat with the hand-held electric whisk until soft and smooth.

18. Sieve in the icing sugar and add the vanilla extract.

19. Add a little more than half of the caramel sauce.

20. Beat the mixture with the electric whisk for 1–2 minutes until light and fluffy.

21. Place the piping bag, fitted with a plain nozzle, into a large glass. This will make it easier to add the icing. Fold out the open end of the piping bag, to make a cuff. Spoon the icing into the piping bag. Set the piping bag aside until needed.

 TIP Disposable piping bags are ideal. If they are unavailable, try using a freezer bag. You can snip one corner of the freezer bag to pipe the icing.

Assembly:

22. When the cupcakes are cooked, remove them from the oven. Place the tin on a wire rack and allow the cupcakes to cool in the tin for 3–4 minutes. Then remove the cupcakes from the tin and place them on the wire rack to cool completely.

23. Using a small, sharp knife, cut a small hole in the centre of each cupcake. Set the cut-out section aside until required.

24. Using a small spoon, add some caramel sauce into the centre of each cupcake and top with the cut-out sections you just set aside. Set aside a little sauce to drizzle over the top afterwards.

 TIP Many homeware shops now sell cupcake corers, which make this process simple and easy.

25. Using the piping bag, swirl the buttercream icing onto each cupcake. (Hold the piping bag vertically, with your writing hand at the top and your other hand at the bottom. Starting on the outside of the cupcake, squeeze from the top of the bag and gently swirl the icing in a circular motion until the cupcake is covered. Stop squeezing once you have reached the centre and lift the bag up to finish.)

26. Drizzle the remaining caramel sauce on top of each cupcake and serve.

Chocolate, Orange and Hazelnut Biscotti

SUGGESTED AREAS OF PRACTICE

Area of Practice C: Food Technology | Home Baking: Biscuits

Serves: 4–6

Preparation Time: 30 minutes

Cooking Time: 40–45 minutes

Ingredients:

- 60 g of hazelnuts
- 2 medium eggs
- 125 g of soft light brown sugar
- 60 g of milk or dark chocolate
- 250 g of plain flour
- ½ teaspoon of bicarbonate of soda
- Zest of 1 orange
- ½ teaspoon of vanilla extract

Method:

1. Preheat the oven to 180 °C/160 °C fan/gas mark 4.

2. Line a large baking tray with baking parchment or silicone paper.

3. On a separate baking tray, spread the hazelnuts out in a single layer. Bake in the oven for 10–12 minutes or until they begin to brown and the skin begins to split.

4. While the hazelnuts are roasting, wash the orange and remove the zest using the fine side of the grater.

5. Remove the hazelnuts from the oven and empty them onto a clean tea towel. Rub the roasted hazelnuts until the skins begin to come off.

6. Roughly chop the hazelnuts and set them aside until required.

7. Using a hand-held electric whisk, whisk the eggs, sugar and vanilla extract together in a large mixing bowl until pale and fluffy.

8. Roughly chop the chocolate.

9. Sieve the flour and bicarbonate of soda into another large bowl and add the orange zest, hazelnuts and chocolate.

10. Pour the egg mixture into the dry ingredients and use a wooden spoon to gently mix them together to make a soft dough.

11. Lightly flour the work surface and tip the dough onto it. With lightly floured hands, shape the dough into a 25 cm log.

12. Place the dough on the lined baking tray. Use your hands to flatten it to a 3 cm thickness.

13. Bake for 30 minutes or until lightly browned on top.

14. Remove the log from the oven and slide it onto a chopping board.

15. Reduce the oven to 160 °C /140 °C fan/gas mark 3.

16. Cut the log into 1 cm thick slices. Return these to the baking sheet, cut sides facing up.

17. Bake the biscotti for a further 10–15 minutes, or until they become crisp. Cool the biscotti on a wire rack. They will keep for 3–4 weeks in an airtight container.

CHOCOLATE, ORANGE AND HAZELNUT BISCOTTI

Diabetic-friendly Carrot and Walnut Cake

SUGGESTED AREAS OF PRACTICE

Area of Practice A: Application of Nutritional Principles | Diabetic

Area of Practice C: Food Technology | Home Baking

Serves: 10
Preparation Time: 25 minutes
Cooking Time: 30 minutes

Ingredients:

For the cake:

- 2 teaspoons of butter (for greasing)
- 1 cooking apple
- 50 ml of water
- 50 g of walnuts
- 2 medium carrots
- Zest of ½ an orange
- 200 g of self-raising flour
- 1 teaspoon of baking powder
- ½ teaspoon of salt
- 1 teaspoon of ground cinnamon
- ½ teaspoon of ground allspice
- 75 g of artificial sweetener
- 4 eggs
- 100 ml of maple syrup
- 1 teaspoon of vanilla extract

For the icing:

- 2 tablespoons of orange juice
- 1 × 180 g tub of cream cheese
- 1 tablespoon of maple syrup
- 2 teaspoons of vanilla extract
- Zest of ½ an orange

To decorate:

- 25 g of walnut halves

Method:

Cake:

1. Preheat the oven to 200 °C/180 °C fan/gas mark 6.
2. Grease a 20 cm x 30 cm rectangular tin with the butter and line the base with baking parchment or silicone paper.
3. Peel and core the apple and chop it roughly. Put it in a saucepan with the water and place the saucepan on a high heat for 5–6 minutes, or until the apple has broken down and formed a sauce. Monitor this carefully, as you may need to add a little more water during cooking. When it is done, set it aside until required.
4. Roughly chop the walnuts.
5. Top and tail the carrots. Then peel them and grate them using the fine side of the grater.
6. Wash the orange. Remove the zest, using the fine side of the grater. Keep half of the zest for the cake and set aside the other half for the icing.
7. Sieve the flour and baking powder into a large mixing bowl. Add the salt, cinnamon, allspice, sweetener and the orange zest you set aside.
8. In a jug, beat the eggs using a whisk or fork. Add the maple syrup, vanilla extract and 3 tablespoons of the apple sauce, and mix.
9. Pour the wet ingredients into the dry ingredients and gently mix with a wooden spoon.
10. Add the carrots and walnuts and gently stir them into the batter until combined.
11. Pour the batter into the tin and bake in the oven for 30 minutes. Insert a skewer or sharp knife into the cake. If it comes out clean, the cake is done.

> **Did you know** ?
>
> Studies have shown that maple syrup may be beneficial for those with diabetes because it contains substances called polyphenols. Polyphenols are thought to inhibit enzymes involved in the conversion of carbohydrate to sugar. This might help control blood sugar levels.

Icing:

12. While the carrot cake is baking, make the icing.
13. Squeeze the juice of half the orange, using a juicer.
14. Put the cream cheese, maple syrup and vanilla extract into a bowl.
15. Add the orange zest you set aside earlier and two tablespoons of the orange juice.
16. Beat well with a wooden spoon until the icing is smooth.

Assembly:

17. Remove the cake from the oven. Place the tin on a wire rack and allow the cake to cool in the tin for 5 minutes.
18. Remove the cake from the tin and place it back on the wire rack to cool completely.
19. When the cake has cooled completely, spread the icing onto the surface of the cake using a palette knife.
20. Decorate the cake with the walnut halves.
21. To serve, cut into even-sized squares and place on a serving plate.

DIABETIC-FRIENDLY CARROT AND WALNUT CAKE

Cranberry and Orange Scones with Orange Butter

SUGGESTED AREAS OF PRACTICE

Area of Practice C: Food Technology | Home Baking

Serves: Makes 15–18 scones
Preparation Time: 20 minutes
Cooking Time: 15 minutes

Ingredients:

For the scones:
- 600 g of plain white flour, plus extra for dusting
- Zest of ½ an orange
- ¼ teaspoon of salt
- 2 heaped teaspoons of baking powder
- 40 g of caster sugar
- 120 g of butter
- 50 g of dried cranberries
- 2 eggs, plus 1 to glaze
- 300 ml of milk

For the orange butter:
- Zest of ½ an orange
- 120 g of butter, at room temperature
- 150 g of icing sugar
- 1 tablespoon of orange juice

To garnish:
- 2 teaspoons of icing sugar, for dusting

Method:

Scones:

1. Preheat the oven to 200 °C/180 °C fan/gas mark 6.
2. Lightly dust two baking trays with flour.
3. Wash the orange. Remove the zest using the fine side of a grater.
4. Sieve the flour into a large mixing bowl. Add a pinch of salt, the baking powder and the caster sugar.
5. Cut the butter into small cubes. Using your fingertips, rub it into the flour, salt, baking powder and caster sugar until it resembles coarse breadcrumbs.
6. Add the cranberries and half the orange zest to the dry ingredients and mix thoroughly.
7. In a jug, beat 2 of the eggs with the milk using a whisk or fork.
8. Make a well in the centre of the dry ingredients and pour in the beaten eggs and milk.
9. Using a wooden spoon, combine the wet and dry ingredients until they form a dough.
10. Sprinkle the extra flour onto the worktop and turn out the dough. Using your fingertips, lightly shape the dough into a ball.
11. Roll or pat the dough gently into a disc about 2½ cm thick.
12. Using a large scone cutter, cut out scones until all of the dough is used up. You will need to tidy the scraps, re-roll and cut out more scones.
13. Place the scones on the floured baking trays, slightly apart from each other.
14. Beat the remaining egg in a cup and brush it over the top of each scone, to glaze.
15. Bake the scones in the oven for 15 minutes or until golden brown on top. The base of the scones should make a hollow sound when tapped. Place on a wire rack to cool.

Orange butter:

16. While the scones are baking, make the orange butter.
17. In a bowl, add the remaining half of the orange zest to the butter. Using a wooden spoon, beat them together until soft.
18. Sieve in the icing sugar.
19. Squeeze the juice from the orange, using a juicer. Measure out 1 tablespoon of juice and add it to the butter, zest and icing sugar.
20. Use a wooden spoon to beat everything together until light and fluffy.

Final stage:

21. Once the scones have cooled, dust them lightly with the 2 teaspoons of icing sugar.
22. Place a scone on a serving plate and serve with a portion of orange butter.

CRANBERRY AND ORANGE SCONES WITH ORANGE BUTTER

Tomato and Mozzarella Bread

SUGGESTED AREAS OF PRACTICE

Area of Practice B: Food Preparation and Cooking Processes | Yeast

Area of Practice C: Food Technology | Bread

_____

Serves: 6

Preparation Time: 1 hour 30 minutes

Cooking Time: 20–25 minutes

Ingredients:

For the bread:

- 250 g of strong white flour, plus extra for dusting
- A pinch of caster sugar
- 1 teaspoon of salt
- 1 × 7 g sachet of fast-action dried yeast
- 190 ml of tepid water
- 1 tablespoon of olive oil, plus 2 teaspoons for oiling
- 10 cherry tomatoes
- 2 teaspoons of fine semolina for dusting
- 1 × 125 g ball of buffalo mozzarella

For sprinkling on top of the bread:

- 1 tablespoon of olive oil
- 1–2 teaspoons of dried oregano
- Sea salt

Method:

1. Line a baking tray with baking parchment or silicone paper.
2. Sieve the flour into a large mixing bowl and add the sugar.
3. Add the salt to one side of the mixing bowl and the yeast to the other.
4. Place the tepid water in a jug and add in the tablespoon of olive oil. Mix thoroughly, using a fork or whisk.
5. Add ¾ of the water-oil mixture to the flour and mix with a wooden spoon. As the dough begins to come together, slowly add the remaining water until a dough ball is formed and no loose flour remains. You may not need to add all of the water.
6. Lightly flour the work surface and tip out the dough. Using your hands, knead the dough to develop the gluten in the flour. (Stretch out the dough, using one hand to hold part of the dough in place and the other hand to stretch it away from you. Fold the dough back on itself and flatten it. Rotate the dough and repeat the process. Do this for at least 10 minutes.)
7. Roll the dough into a ball.
8. Wash the mixing bowl and lightly oil it with the olive oil.
9. Place the dough in the oiled bowl, cover it with cling film and leave it in a warm place for around 1 hour so the dough can prove and double in size.
10. While the dough is proving, wash the cherry tomatoes. Cut them in half and place in a bowl until needed.
11. After proving is complete and the dough has doubled in size, dust the work surface with a mixture of flour and semolina and carefully tip out the dough. Knock back the dough by kneading briefly and gently to distribute the air bubbles.
12. Cut the dough in half and, with a lightly floured rolling pin, roll each half out carefully to form a large oval about 20 cm in length.
13. Lay the two breads on the baking tray, leaving a gap between them.
14. Push 10 tomato halves into the surface of each bread with the cut sides facing upwards.
15. Snip a hole in the corner of the bag of fresh mozzarella and drain the liquid. Cut the bag open and remove the mozzarella. Tear it into pieces and push the pieces into the dough in the gaps between the tomatoes.
16. Cover the breads with cling film and leave for 15 minutes in a warm place to prove for a second time.
17. Preheat the oven to 200 °C/180 °C fan/gas mark 6.
18. After proving, drizzle both breads with olive oil and sprinkle with oregano and sea salt.
19. Place the bread in the oven and bake for 20–25 minutes or until it is golden brown and the base makes a hollow sound when tapped.
20. Remove the bread from the oven. Place the baking tray on a wire rack and allow the bread to cool on the tray for 5 minutes.
21. Cut the bread into slices and place on a serving plate or board.

TOMATO AND MOZZARELLA BREAD

Sweet or Savoury Tear and Share

Sweet

SUGGESTED AREAS OF PRACTICE

Area of Practice B: Food Preparation and Cooking Processes | Yeast

Area of Practice C: Food Technology | Bread

Serves: 8–10

Preparation Time: 1 hour 45 minutes

Cooking Time: 20–25 minutes

Ingredients:

- 200 ml of milk
- 450 g of strong white flour
- 1 teaspoon of salt
- 1 × 7 g sachet of fast-action dried yeast
- 150 ml of lukewarm water
- 1 tablespoon of honey
- 1 tablespoon of sunflower oil, plus 2 teaspoons for oiling
- 1 egg

Savoury tear and share:

- 25 g of sunflower seeds
- 25 g of poppy seeds
- 25 g of sesame seeds
- 25 g of rolled oats

Sweet tear and share:

- 25 g of butter
- ¼ teaspoon of ground cinnamon
- 55 g of sultanas
- 2 tablespoons of soft light brown sugar

TIP Sultanas can be substituted with dried cranberries or chocolate chips.

In this recipe, you can decide whether you want to make sweet rolls or savoury rolls.

Method:

Dough:

1. Pour the milk into a medium saucepan and heat on a medium heat for 2–3 minutes. Alternatively, put the milk into a jug and microwave on medium power for 20 seconds or until lukewarm.
2. Sieve the flour into a large mixing bowl.
3. Add the salt to one side of the mixing bowl and the yeast to the other.
4. Add the water, honey and sunflower oil to the milk. Mix thoroughly using a fork or whisk.
5. Make a well in the centre of the flour and pour in three-quarters of the liquid. Combine until a slightly wet dough forms. You may not need to add all of the liquid.

6. Lightly flour the work surface and tip out the dough. Using your hands, knead the dough to develop the gluten in the flour. (Stretch out the dough, using one hand to hold part of the dough in place and the other hand to stretch it away from you. Fold the dough back on itself and flatten it. Rotate the dough and repeat the process. Do this for at least 10 minutes.)

7. Clean the mixing bowl and lightly oil it with the sunflower oil.

8. Place the dough into the oiled bowl, cover it with cling film and leave it in a warm place for around 1 hour so the dough can prove and double in size.

9. Using a pastry brush, oil the inside of a square 23 cm springform tin (or a 23 cm × 33 cm rectangular tin) with sunflower oil.

10. After proving is complete and the dough has doubled in size, dust the work surface with a mixture of flour and semolina and tip out the dough. Knock back the dough by kneading briefly and gently to distribute the air bubbles.

» If you are making sweet rolls, skip to step 17.

Savoury topping:

11. Divide the dough into 16 even pieces. (Cut the dough into quarters and then cut each quarter into 4 pieces.)

12. Gently roll each piece into a ball and place in the greased tin. Continue until all 16 balls are in place.

13. Cover the tin loosely with cling film and leave in a warm place for 30 minutes to prove for a second time.

14. Preheat the oven to 200 °C/180 °C fan/gas mark 6.

15. Beat the egg in a cup. Brush the beaten egg over each dough ball using a pastry brush, to glaze.

16. Sprinkle each type of seed over 4 balls (e.g. 4 balls with sunflower seeds, 4 with poppy seeds, 4 with sesame seeds and 4 with rolled oats.) Alternate the toppings so that each roll is different.

» Skip to step 27.

Sweet filling:

17. Roll out the dough into a large rectangular shape, 30 cm × 20 cm.

18. Melt the butter in a saucepan on a low heat for 1 minute, or microwave on medium power for 30 seconds. Add the cinnamon. Stir well using a fork or whisk.

19. Brush the dough with the melted butter.

20. Sprinkle the sultanas and brown sugar evenly over the dough.

21. Starting on the 30 cm (long) side, roll up the dough like a Swiss roll.

22. Slice the roll into 2½ cm pieces (approx. 16 pieces).

23. Arrange the pieces, swirl side up, in the oiled tin.

24. Cover the tin loosely with cling film and leave in a warm place for 30 minutes to prove for a second time.

25. Preheat the oven to 200 °C/180 °C fan/gas mark 6.

26. Beat the egg in a cup and brush it over each swirl, to glaze.

Final stage:

27. Place the bread in the oven and bake for 20–25 minutes or until it is golden brown and the base makes a hollow sound when tapped.

28. Remove the bread from the oven. Place the tin on a wire rack and allow the bread to cool in the tin for 5 minutes.

29. Remove the bread from the tin and place on a serving plate or board to serve.

SWEET OR SAVOURY TEAR AND SHARE

Mixed Vegetable Piccalilli

SUGGESTED AREAS OF PRACTICE

Area of Practice C: Food Technology | Pickling

Serves: Yields approximately 2–3 × 454 g jars
Preparation Time: 1 hour 20 minutes
Cooking Time: 20 minutes

Ingredients:

- ½ a large cauliflower
- 1 courgette
- 1 × 200 g packet of fresh green beans
- 2 red chillies
- 1 green chilli
- 4 shallots
- 1 red onion
- 100 g of fine sea salt
- 1 mango
- 2 cloves of garlic
- 1 tablespoon of vegetable oil
- 1 heaped tablespoon of mustard seeds
- 1 tablespoon of ground cumin
- 1 tablespoon of turmeric
- ½ a tablespoon of ground nutmeg
- 1 tablespoon of English mustard powder
- 2 tablespoons of flour
- 250 ml of white wine vinegar
- 100 ml of water
- 1 cooking apple
- 3 tablespoons of caster sugar
- 1 tablespoon of dried oregano
- 1 bay leaf (dried or fresh)

Equipment needed:

- 2–3 × 454 g jars with plastic-coated metal lids
- 1 waxed disc per jar

TIP Always use plastic coated metal lids to prevent the vinegar from reacting with the metal.

Method:

Piccalilli:

1. Wash the cauliflower, courgette and green beans.
2. Chop or break the cauliflower into very small florets. (Make sure they are small enough to fit in the jar.)
3. Chop off each end of the courgette. Then cut it into small chunks.
4. Remove the stalks from the red and green chillies and finely slice the chillies. Do not remove the seeds.
5. Top and tail the green beans and chop into 1 cm lengths.
6. Top and tail the shallots, remove the skin and cut into eighths.
7. Top and tail the red onion, remove the skin and chop roughly into small pieces.
8. Place all of the prepared vegetables in a large mixing bowl and add the salt and enough water to cover completely.
9. Refrigerate the vegetables for at least an hour. It is best to leave them in the fridge overnight to draw the water out of the vegetables.
10. Cut the mango lengthwise to remove the mango cheeks on either side of the centre stone. (Using a sharp knife, make lengthwise and crosswise cuts into the flesh of each mango cheek, being careful not to go through the skin. Press the skin side, so the chunks of flesh poke out. Then trim the chunks off with a sharp knife.)
11. Peel and finely chop or crush the garlic.
12. Preheat a large saucepan over a high heat for 1 minute and add the vegetable oil.
13. Add the mustard seeds, cumin, turmeric and nutmeg to the saucepan. Heat for 1–2 minutes or until the mustard seeds start to pop.
14. Lower the heat to medium and add the mustard powder, flour and 25 ml of the vinegar. Stir well to make a thick paste.
15. Gradually add the remaining vinegar and the water, stirring all the time. When a smooth paste is formed, remove the saucepan from the heat.
16. Remove the vegetables from the fridge and drain them, using a colander. Rinse under the tap for 1–2 minutes to remove the salt water. Set aside until required.
17. Peel the apple and grate using the coarse side of the grater.
18. Place the saucepan back on a medium heat. Add the apples, mango, sugar, garlic, oregano and bay leaf and cook for 2–3 minutes, stirring all the time.
19. Add the drained vegetables to the pan, stirring well to coat with the spicy paste.
20. Cook for 10–15 minutes or until the vegetables have just softened and started to release some juice.

TIP By salting the vegetables first, you ensure that they remain crunchy when cooked.

Potting:

21. As the vegetables are cooking, preheat the oven to 140 °C/120 °C fan/gas mark 1.
22. Wash the jars and their plastic-coated lids in hot, soapy water. Remove any labels. Rinse well.
23. Place the open jars and their lids on a baking tray. Place in the oven for 20 minutes.
24. When the vegetables have softened, remove the saucepan from the heat and allow the contents to cool slightly.
25. Remove the sterilised jars and lids from the oven.
26. Spoon the piccalilli into the jars, leaving a 3 mm space at the top.
27. Gently tap the jars on the counter to remove any air bubbles. Place a waxed disc directly on top of the piccalilli and screw the lids on tightly.
28. Label the jars with the name and date of manufacture.
29. Allow the piccalilli to mature for 2 months. If sealed correctly, the piccalilli will last for 1 year, unopened. Once opened, refrigerate and consume within 2 weeks.

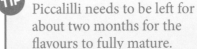

TIP Piccalilli needs to be left for about two months for the flavours to fully mature.

MIXED VEGETABLE PICCALILLI

Spiced Apple and Tomato Chutney

SUGGESTED AREAS OF PRACTICE

Area of Practice C: Food Technology | Chutney

Serves: Yields approximately 2–3 × 454 g jars

Preparation Time: 20–25 minutes

Cooking Time: 1 hour

Ingredients:

- 1.7 kg of ripe tomatoes (approx. 10 large tomatoes)
- 225 g of onions (approx. 3 medium onions)
- 2 cloves of garlic
- 225 g of cooking apples (approx. 1 large cooking apple)
- 450 ml of white malt vinegar
- 650 g of light soft brown sugar
- 1 tablespoon of salt
- 1 teaspoon of ground ginger
- 1 teaspoon of ground black pepper
- 1½ teaspoons of ground allspice
- ½ teaspoon of cayenne pepper
- 175 g sultanas

Equipment needed:
- 2–3 × 454 g jars with plastic-coated metal lids
- 1 waxed disc per jar
- Jam funnel

Method:

Chutney:

1. Boil a full kettle.

2. Wash the tomatoes. Score a shallow X into the bottom of each tomato.

3. Pour the boiling water into a saucepan. Place the saucepan on a high heat and bring the water back to the boil. Fill a large bowl with cold water and place it beside the saucepan. Gently place the tomatoes in the saucepan and leave them for 30 seconds, until the skin begins to peel away.

4. Using a slotted spoon, remove the tomatoes and place in the bowl of cold water to cool down.

5. Remove the tomatoes, gently peel off the skin and chop them into 1 cm pieces.

6. Top and tail the onions, remove the skin and chop roughly into small pieces.

7. Peel and finely chop or crush the garlic.

8. Peel the cooking apples, core them, and chop into 1 cm pieces.

9. Place the tomatoes, onions, garlic and apples in a large, heavy, shallow saucepan.

10. Add the vinegar, sugar, salt, ginger, pepper, allspice, cayenne pepper and sultanas. Stir to combine.

11. Place on a high heat and bring the mixture to the boil.

12. When it has come to the boil, reduce the heat to medium and simmer steadily for around 1 hour (depending on the width and depth of the saucepan used) or until the mixture has reduced and thickened slightly. It should have a jam-like consistency. Keep a watchful eye on the mixture.

 TIP A shallow saucepan will allow evaporation to take place, thickening and reducing the chutney.

Potting:

13. As the vegetables are simmering, preheat the oven to 140 °C/120 °C fan/gas mark 1.

14. Wash the jars and their plastic-coated lids in hot, soapy water. Remove any labels. Rinse well.

15. Place the open jars and their lids on a baking tray. Place in the oven for 20 minutes.

TIP Always use plastic coated metal lids to prevent the vinegar from reacting with the metal.

16. When the chutney has reduced and thickened, remove the pan from the heat.

17. Remove the sterilised jars and lids from the oven.

18. Spoon the chutney into the jars, leaving a 3 mm space at the top. You can also use a jam funnel to pour the chutney into the jars.

19. Gently tap the jars on the counter to remove any air pockets. Place a waxed disc directly on top of the chutney and screw the lids on tightly.

20. Label with the name and date of manufacture.

21. Allow the chutney to mature for 2 weeks before using. If sealed correctly, the chutney will last for 1 year, unopened. Once opened, refrigerate and consume within 2 weeks.

SPICED APPLE AND TOMATO CHUTNEY

Cherry Tomato Chilli Relish

SUGGESTED AREAS OF PRACTICE

Area of Practice C: Food Technology | Relish

Serves: Yields approximately 2–3 × 454 g jars

Preparation Time: 20 minutes

Cooking Time: 1 hour

Ingredients:

- 125 g of onions (approx. 2 medium onions)
- 500 g of cherry tomatoes
- 1 green chilli
- 125g of cooking apples (approx. 1 medium cooking apple)
- 85 g of raisins
- 150 g of caster sugar
- 1 teaspoon of salt
- 115 ml of white wine vinegar
- 1 teaspoon of ground allspice
- ¼ teaspoon of ground ginger
- ¼ teaspoon of ground black pepper
- ¼ teaspoon of cayenne pepper
- ½ teaspoon of ground nutmeg

Equipment needed:

- 2–3 × 454 g jars with plastic-coated metal lids
- 1 waxed disc per jar (size will depend on the size of the jar)
- Jam funnel

Method:

Relish:

1. Top and tail the onions, remove the skin and dice finely.
2. Wash the cherry tomatoes and chop into quarters.
3. Remove the stalk of the chilli, cut lengthwise, remove the seeds and membrane, and dice finely.
4. Peel the cooking apples, core them, and chop into 1 cm pieces.
5. Place the onions, cherry tomatoes, chilli and cooking apples in a large saucepan.
6. Add the raisins, sugar, salt, vinegar, allspice, ginger, black pepper, cayenne pepper and nutmeg.
7. Place the saucepan on a high heat and bring the mixture to the boil.
8. When the mixture has come to the boil, reduce the heat to medium and simmer steadily for around 1 hour (depending on the width and depth of the saucepan used) or until the mixture has reduced and thickened slightly. It should have a jam-like consistency. Keep a watchful eye on the mixture.

Potting:

9. As the vegetables are simmering, preheat the oven to 140 °C/120 °C fan/gas mark 1.
10. Wash the jars and their plastic-coated lids in hot, soapy water. Remove any labels. Rinse well.
11. Place the open jars and their lids on a baking tray. Place in the oven for 20 minutes.

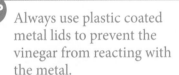

TIP Always use plastic coated metal lids to prevent the vinegar from reacting with the metal.

12. Remove the sterilised jars and lids from the oven.
13. When the relish has reduced and thickened, remove it from the heat.
14. Spoon the relish into the jars. You can also use a jam funnel to pour the relish into the jars.
15. Gently tap the jars on the counter to remove any air pockets. Place a waxed disc directly on top of the relish and screw the lids on tightly.
16. Label with the name and date of manufacture.
17. Allow the relish to mature for 2 weeks before using. If sealed correctly, the relish will last for 1 year, unopened. Once opened, refrigerate and consume within 2 weeks.

CHERRY TOMATO CHILLI RELISH

Blackberry and Apple Jam

Ingredients:

- 1.1 kg of blackberries
- 1 small lemon
- 500 g of cooking apples
  (approx. 2 large cooking apples)
- 125 ml of water
- 1 kg of sugar

Equipment needed:

- 2–3 × 454 g jam jars
- 1 waxed disc per jar (size will
  depend on the size of the jar)
- Cellophane jam pot covers
- Elastic bands
- Jam funnel